I'm grateful to God for everything! And I believe that the meaning of life is to give meaning to other lives. Luciana, you are the meaning of my life.
I love you

Ivani Ribeiro

2024

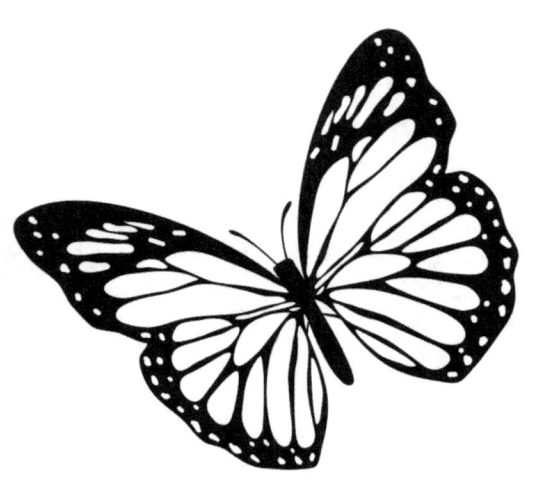 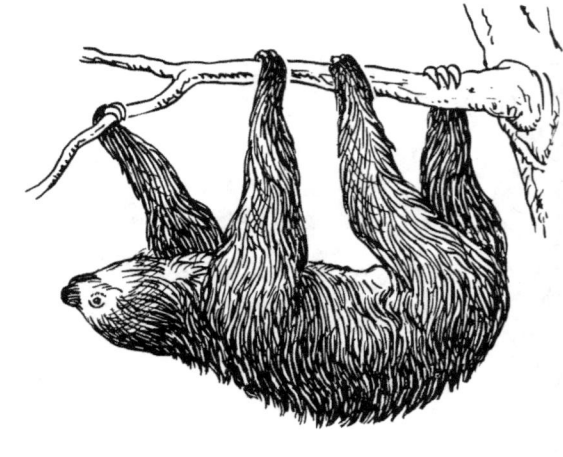

This Book Belongs to:

○──○

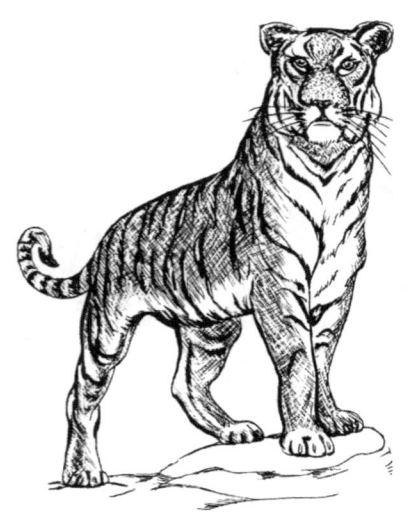 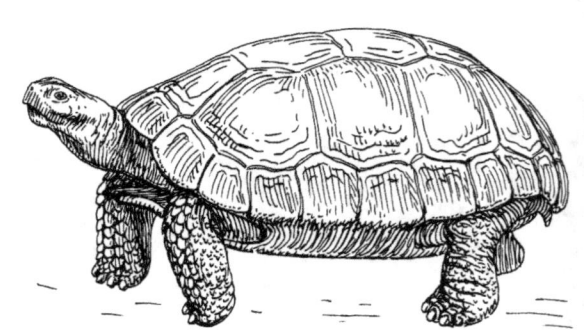

ALL RIGHTS RESERVED©
2024

No part of this publication may be reproduced, distributed, or transmitted in any form or by any means, including photocopying, recording, or other electronic or mechanical methods, without the prior written permission of the publisher, except for brief quotations incorporated in critical reviews and other specific noncommercial uses. Any unauthorized replica of this work is prohibited.

©

I.R.
Ivani's Ribeiro publications

Test Color Page

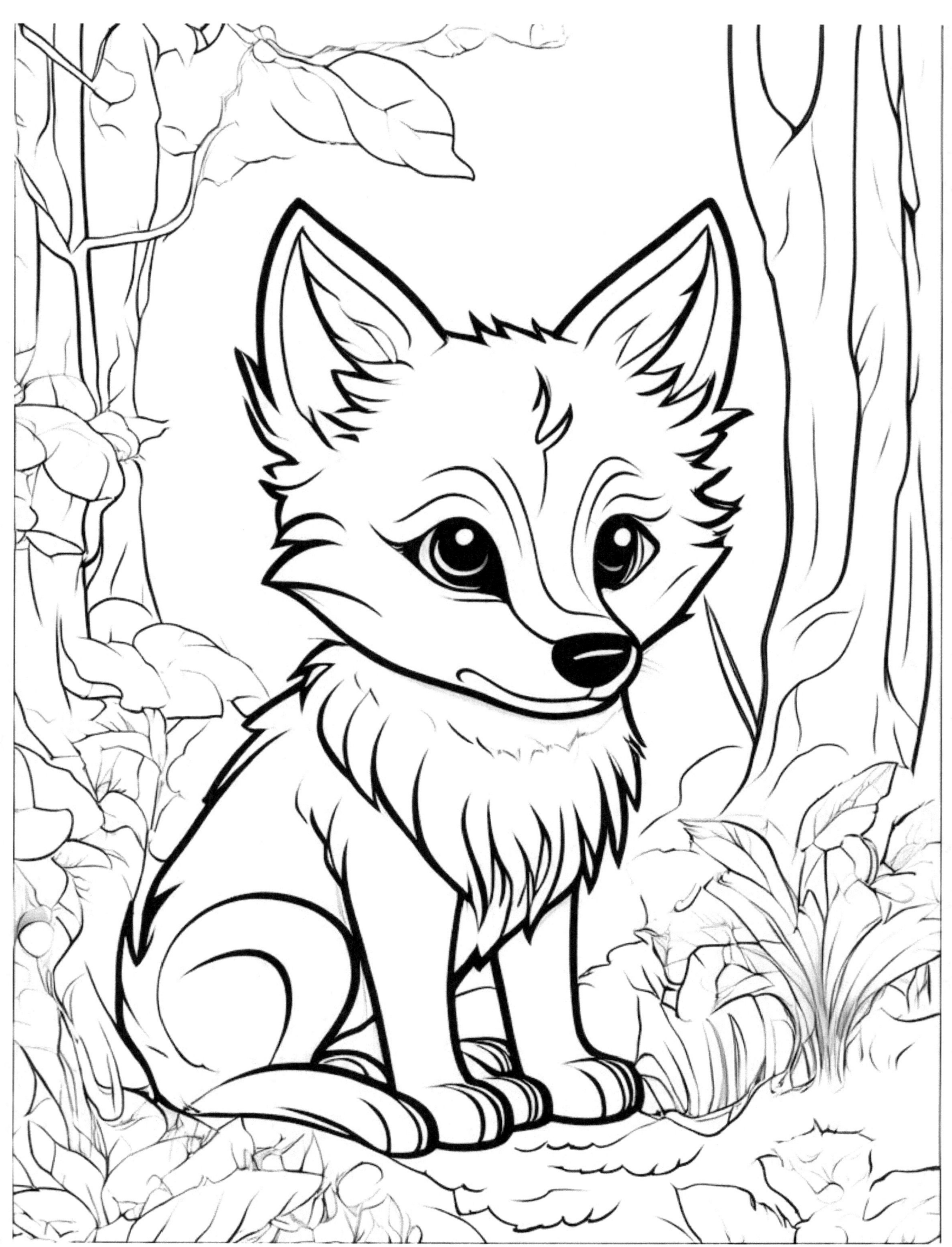

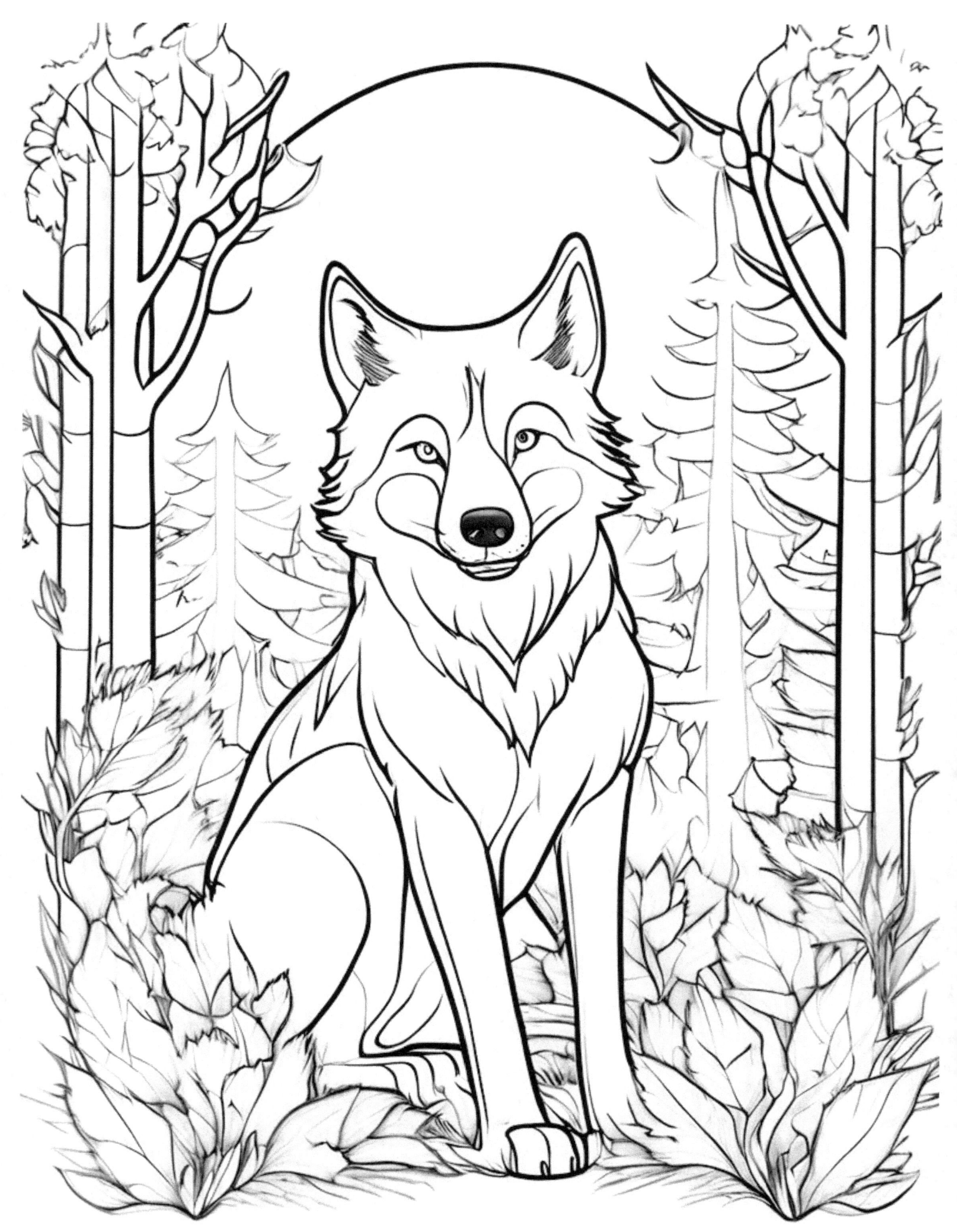

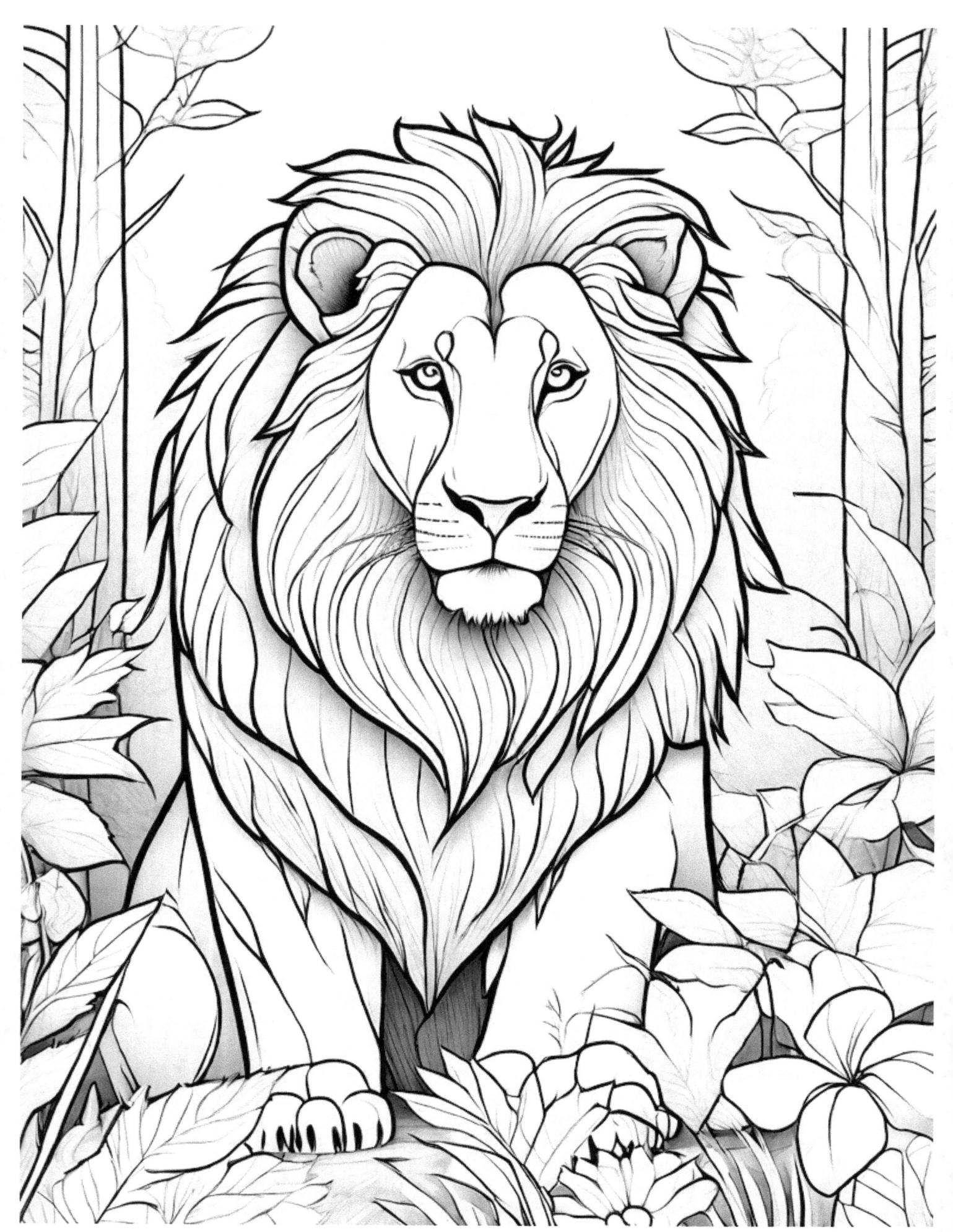

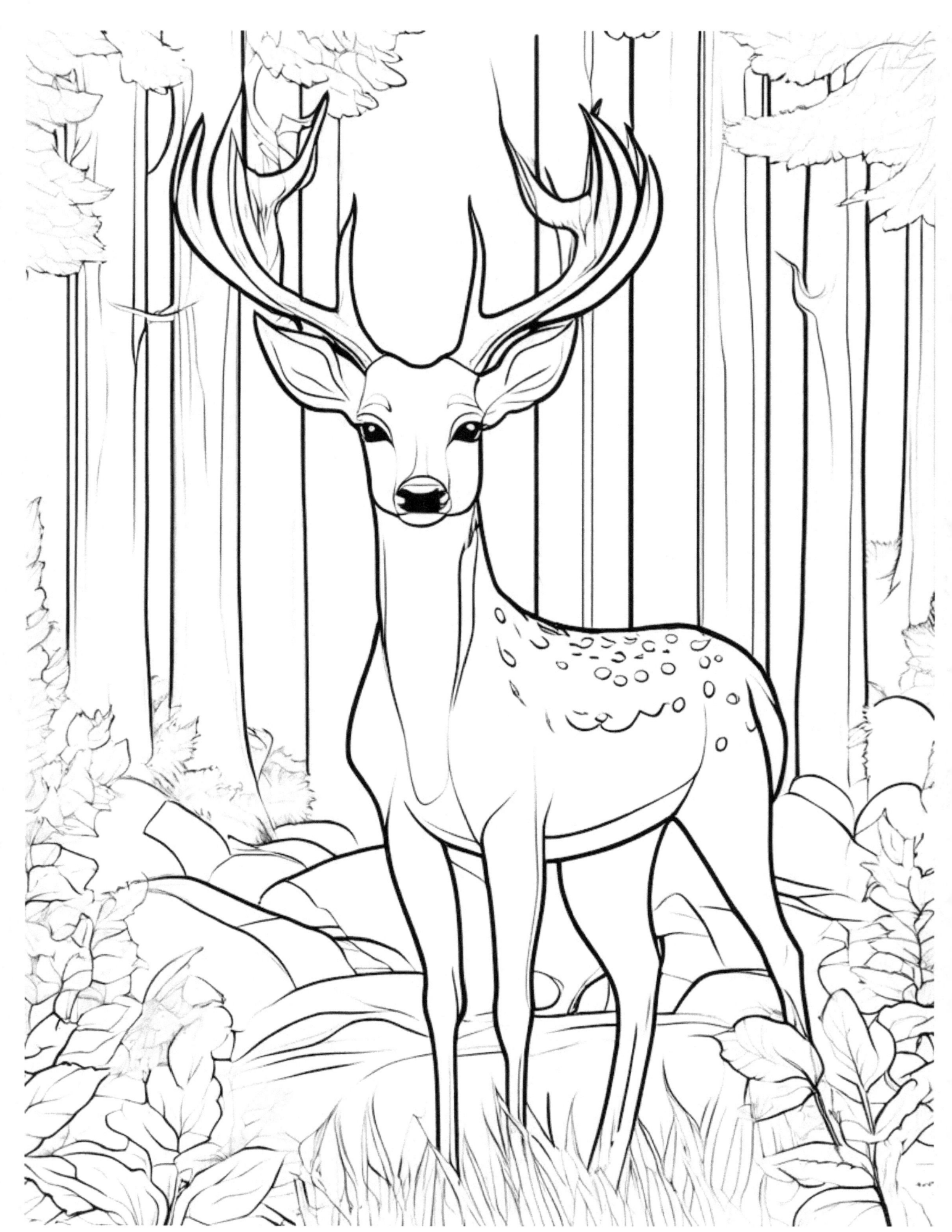

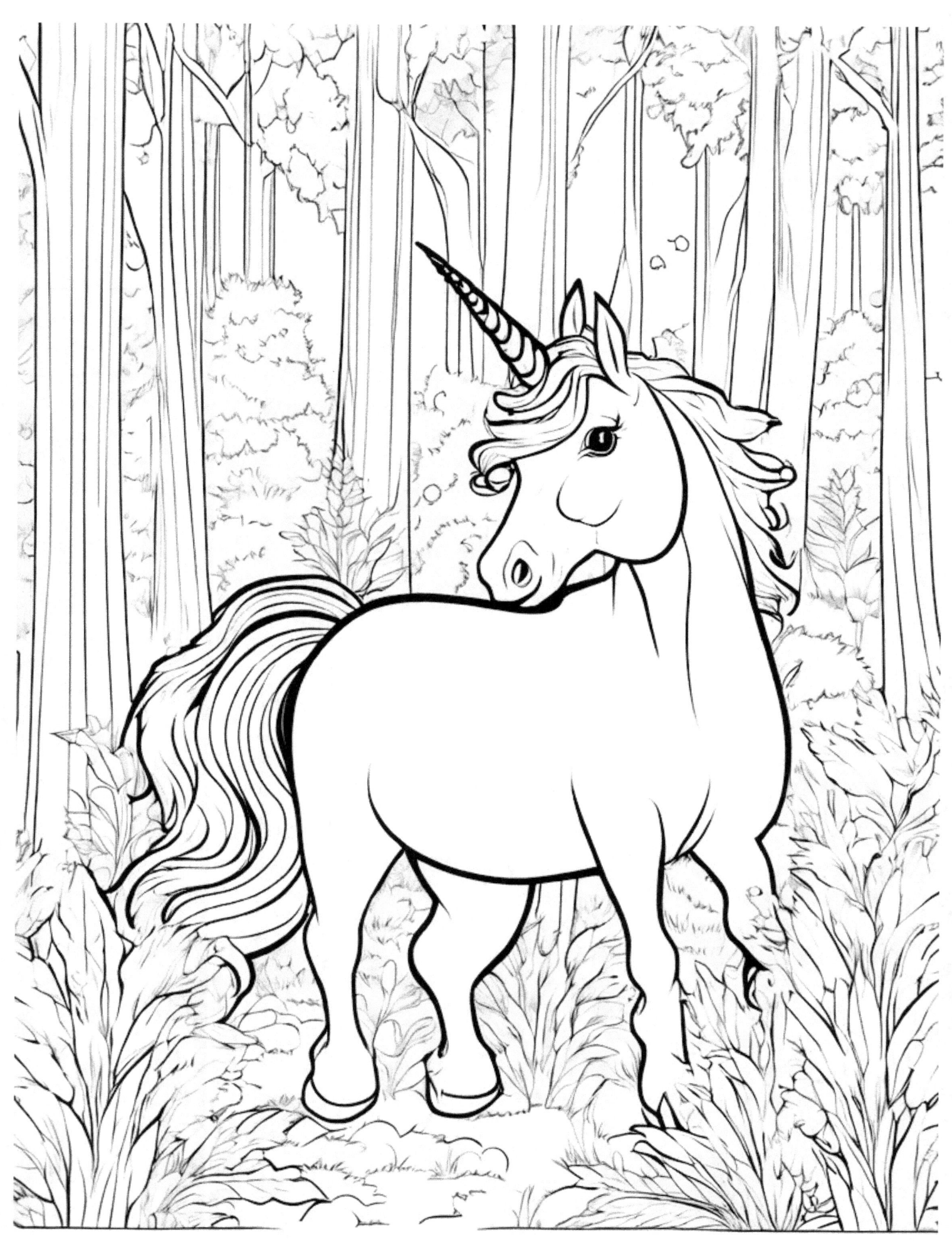

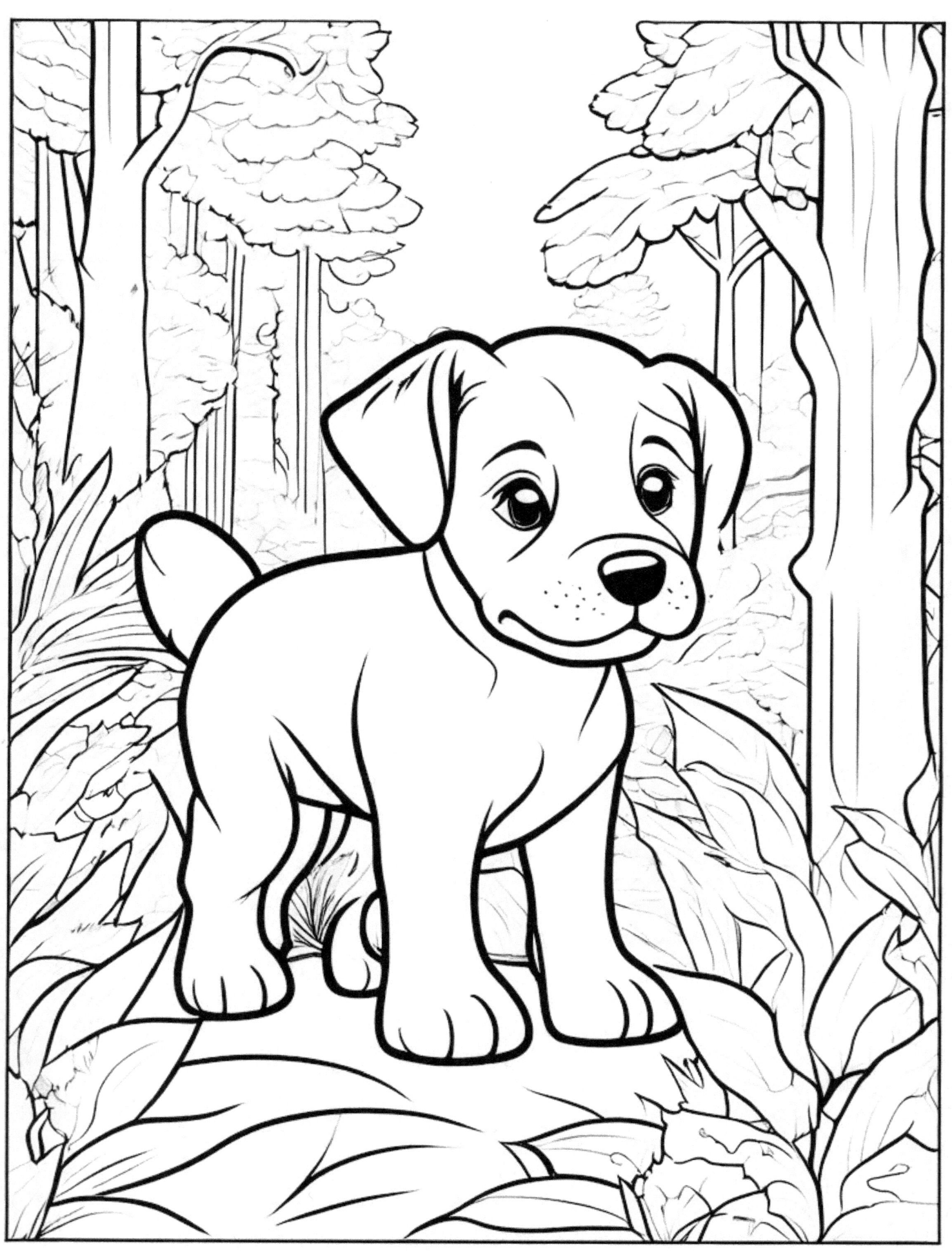

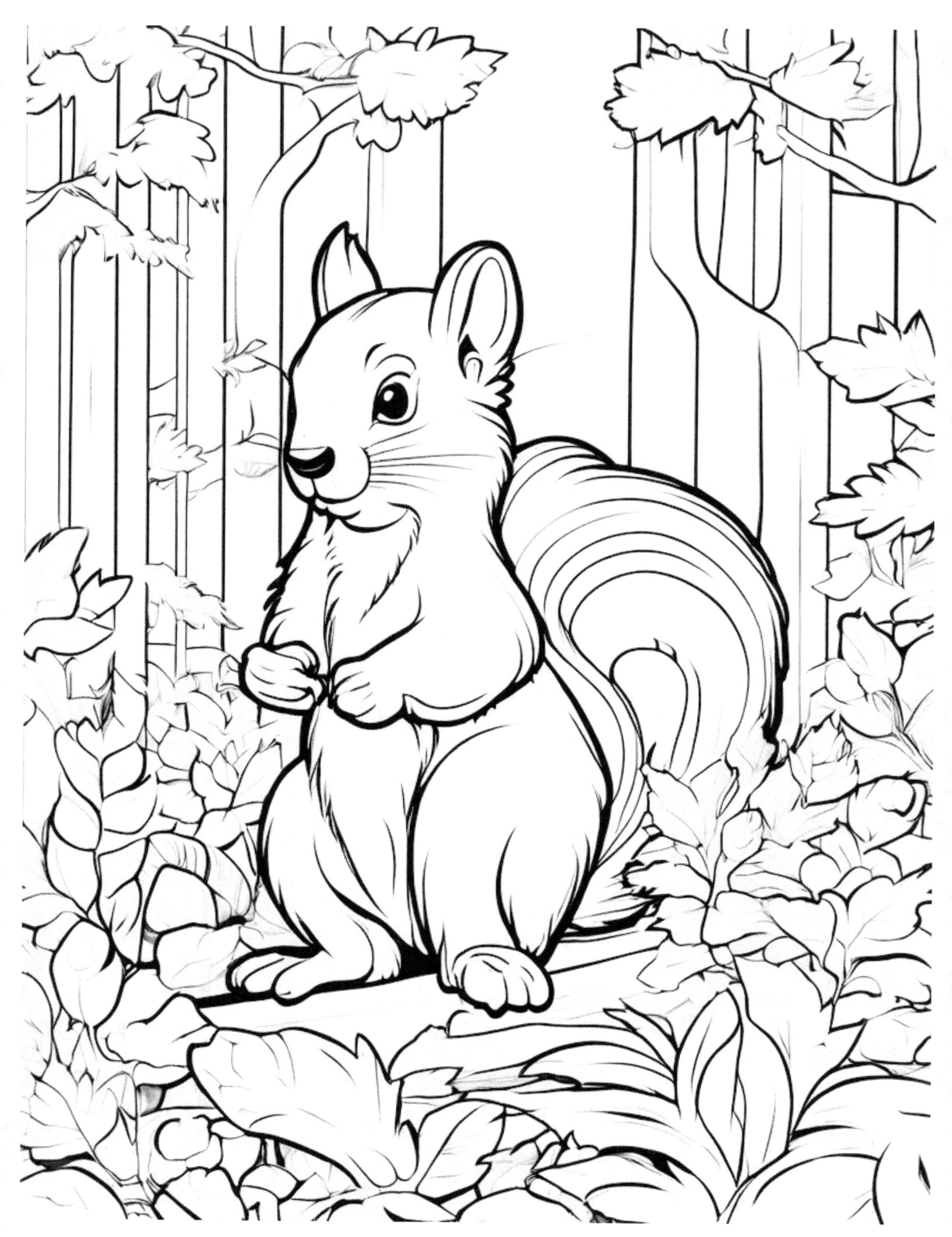

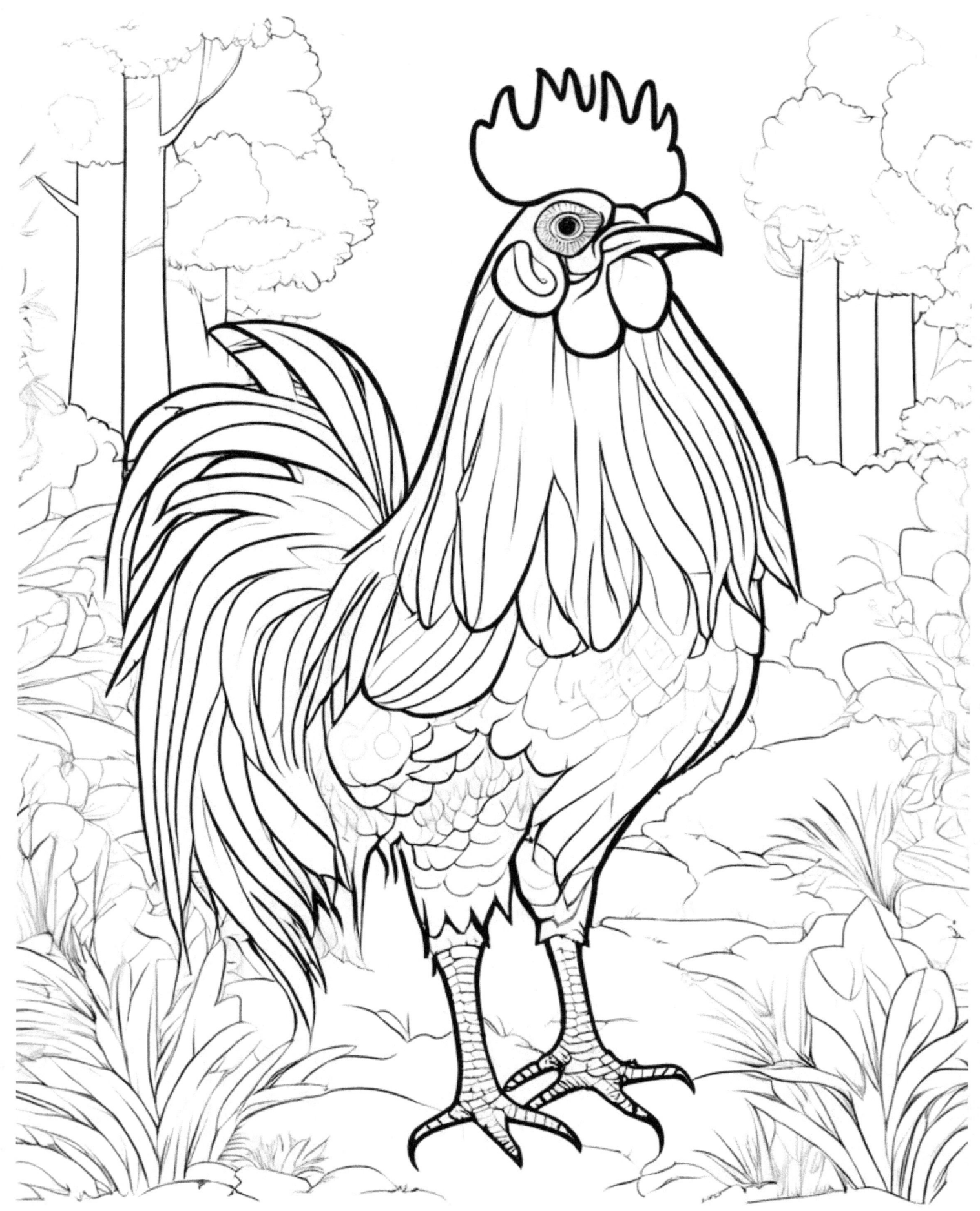

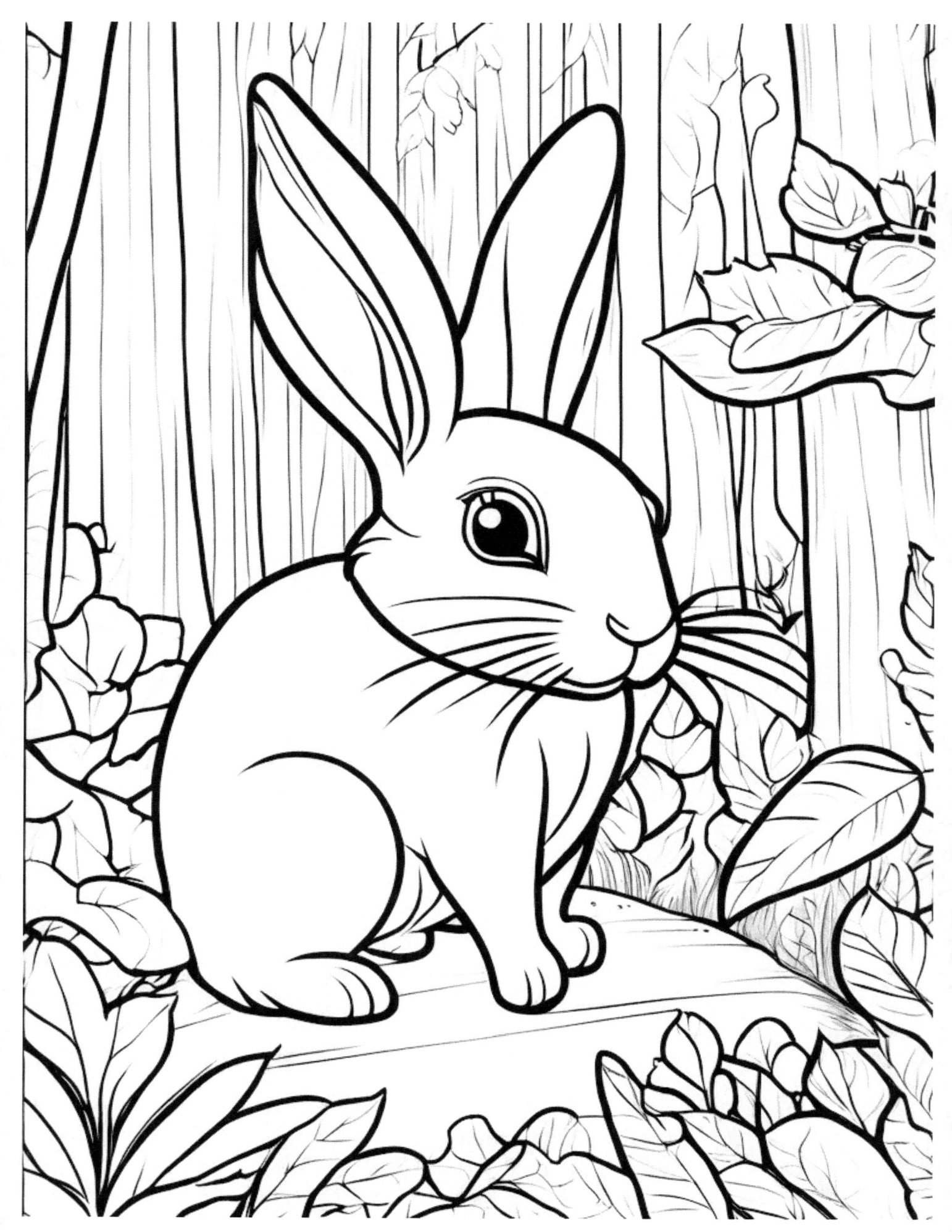

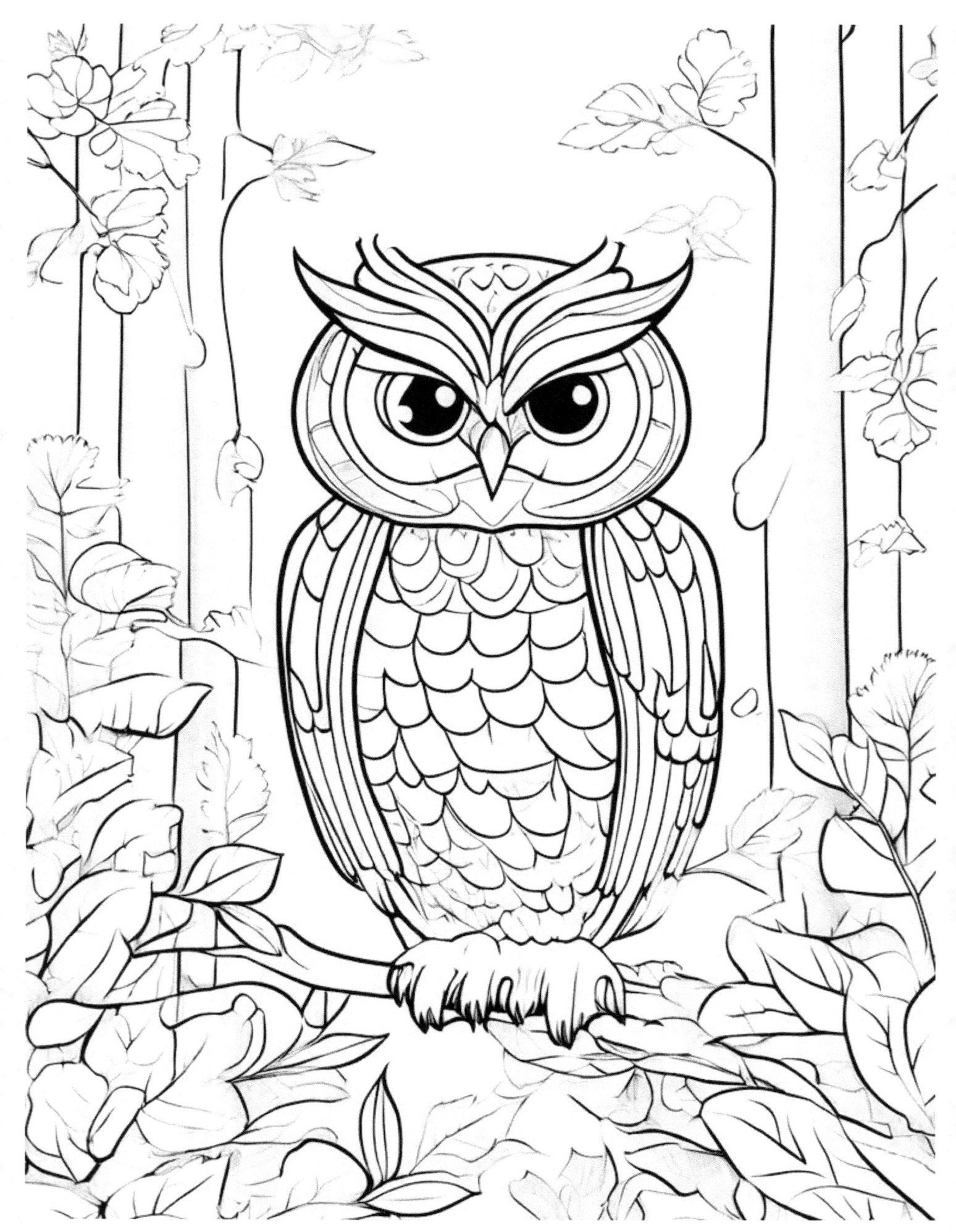

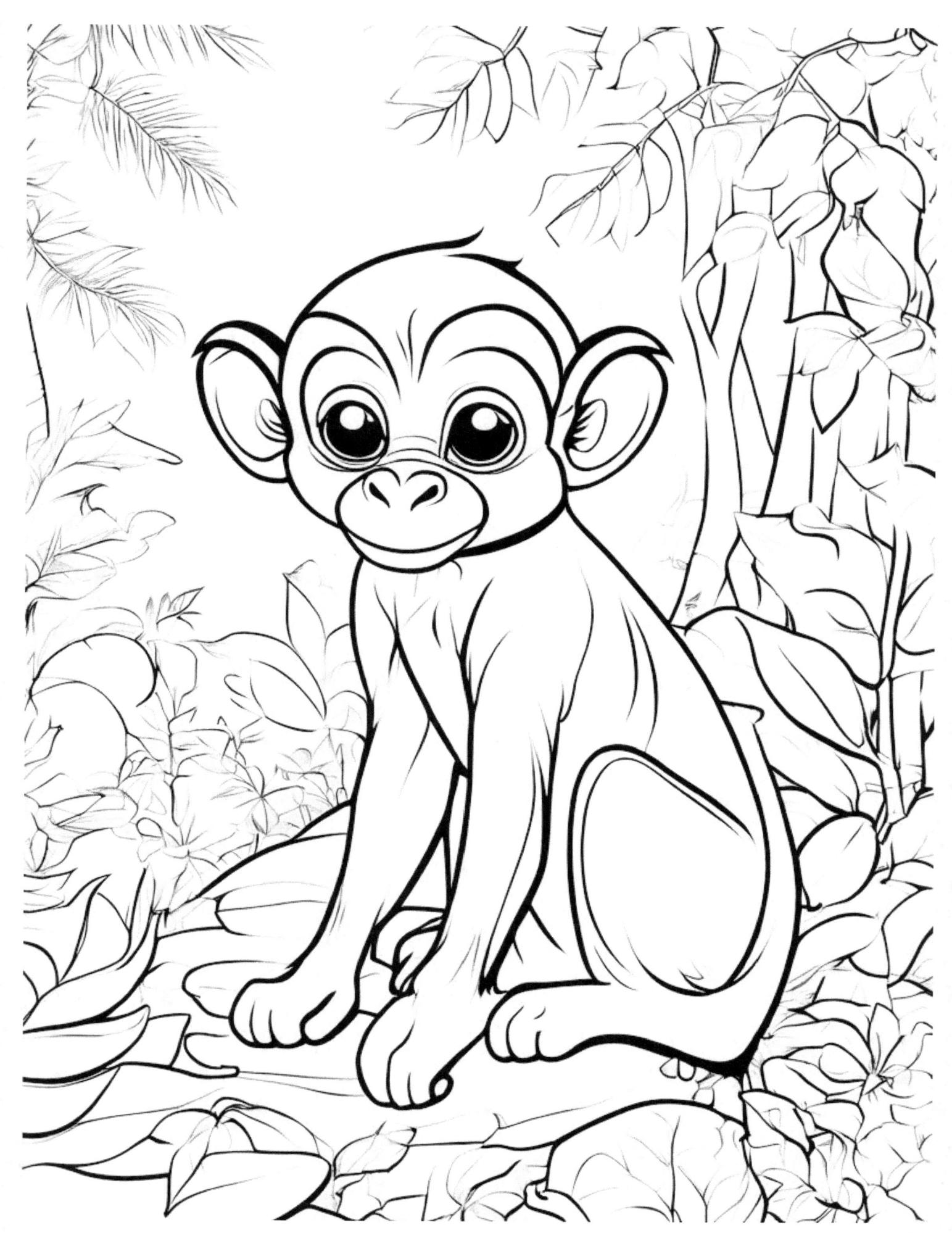

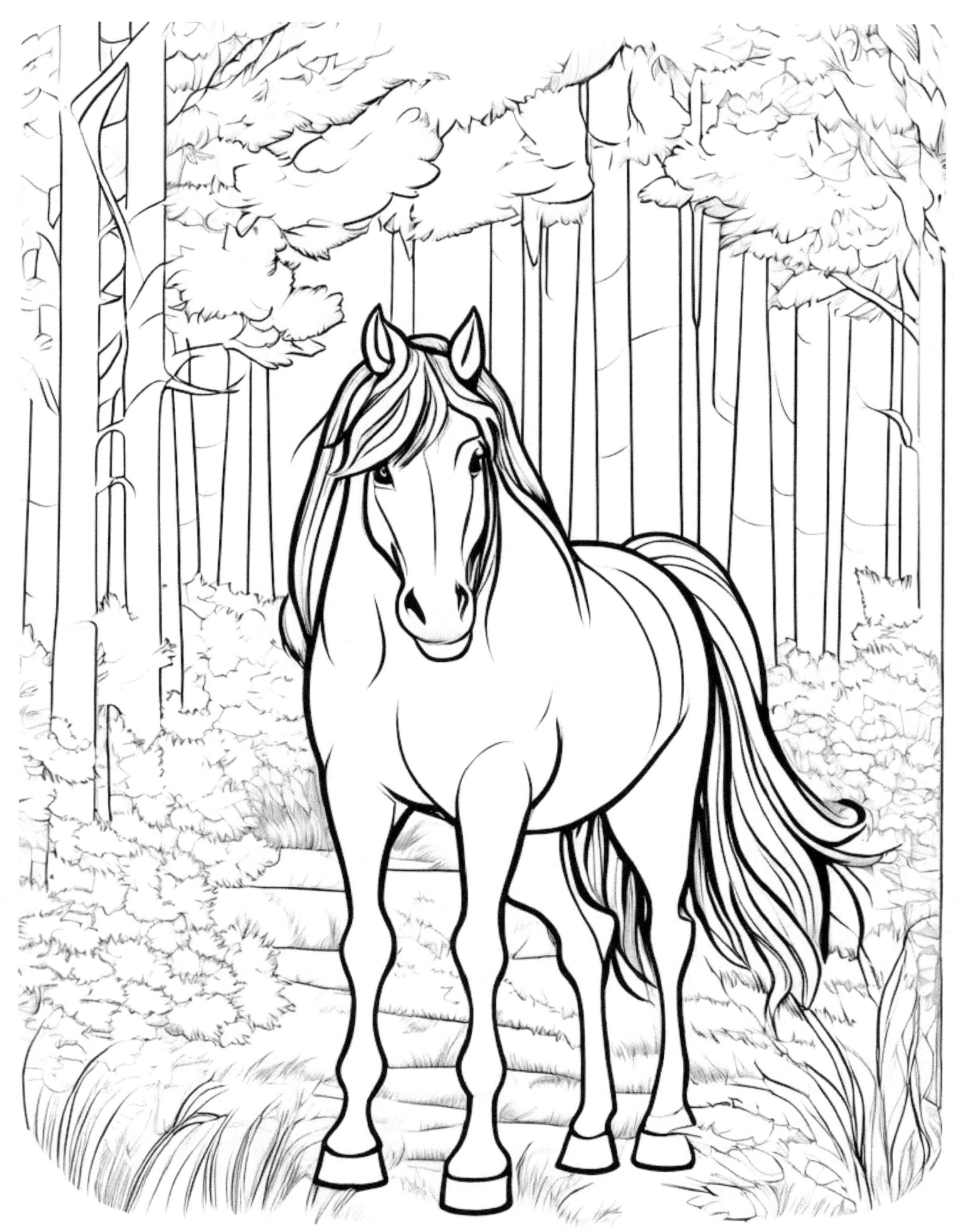

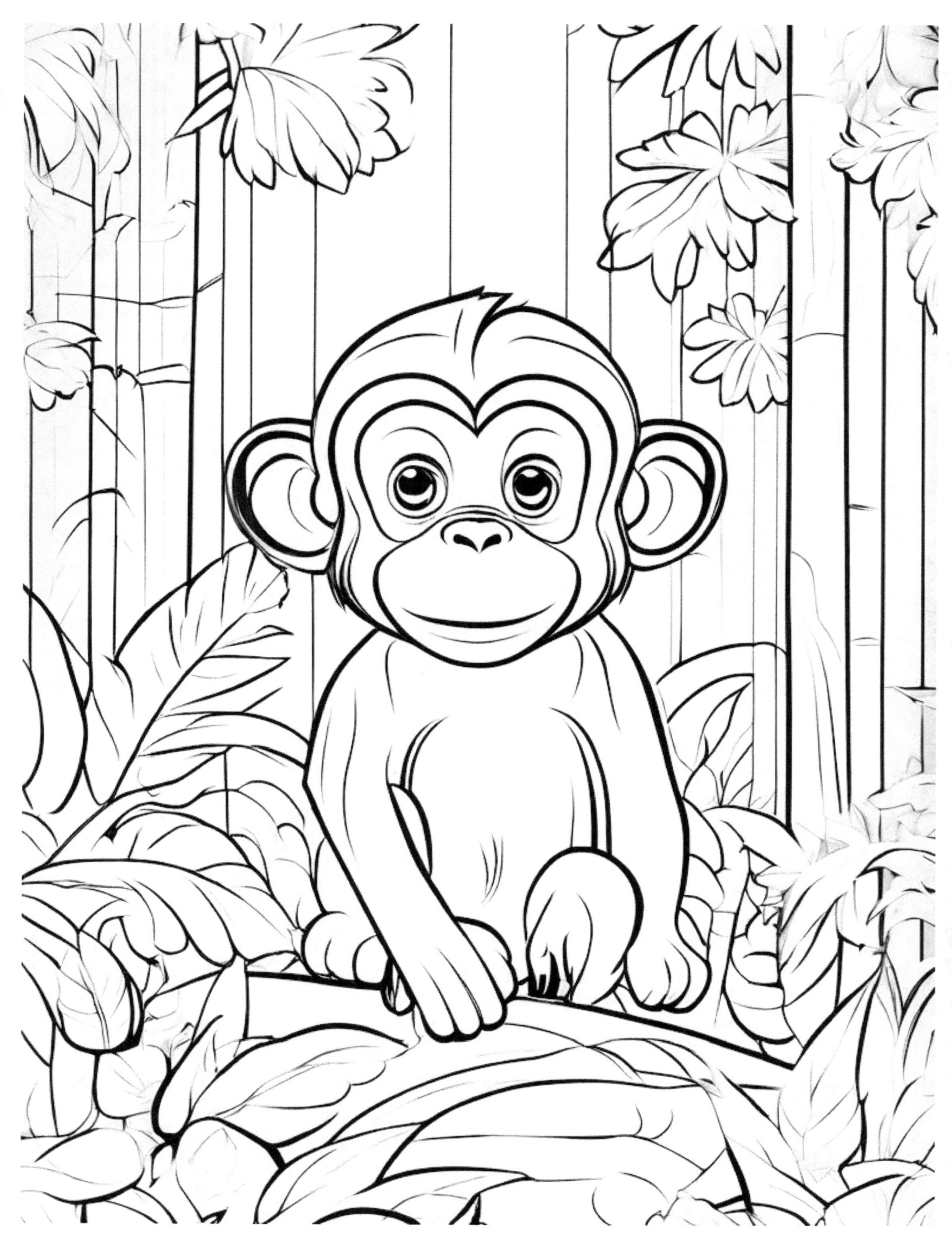

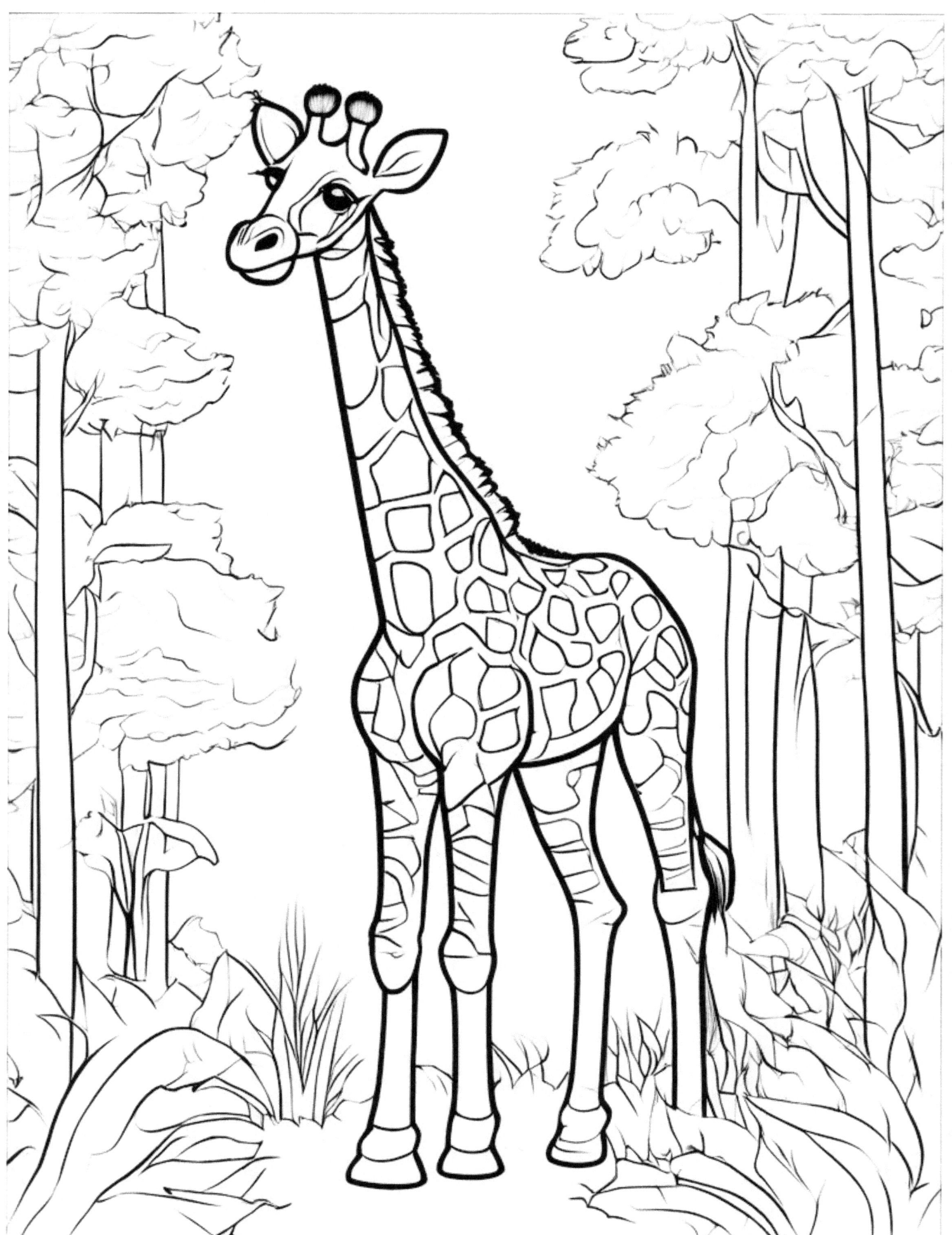

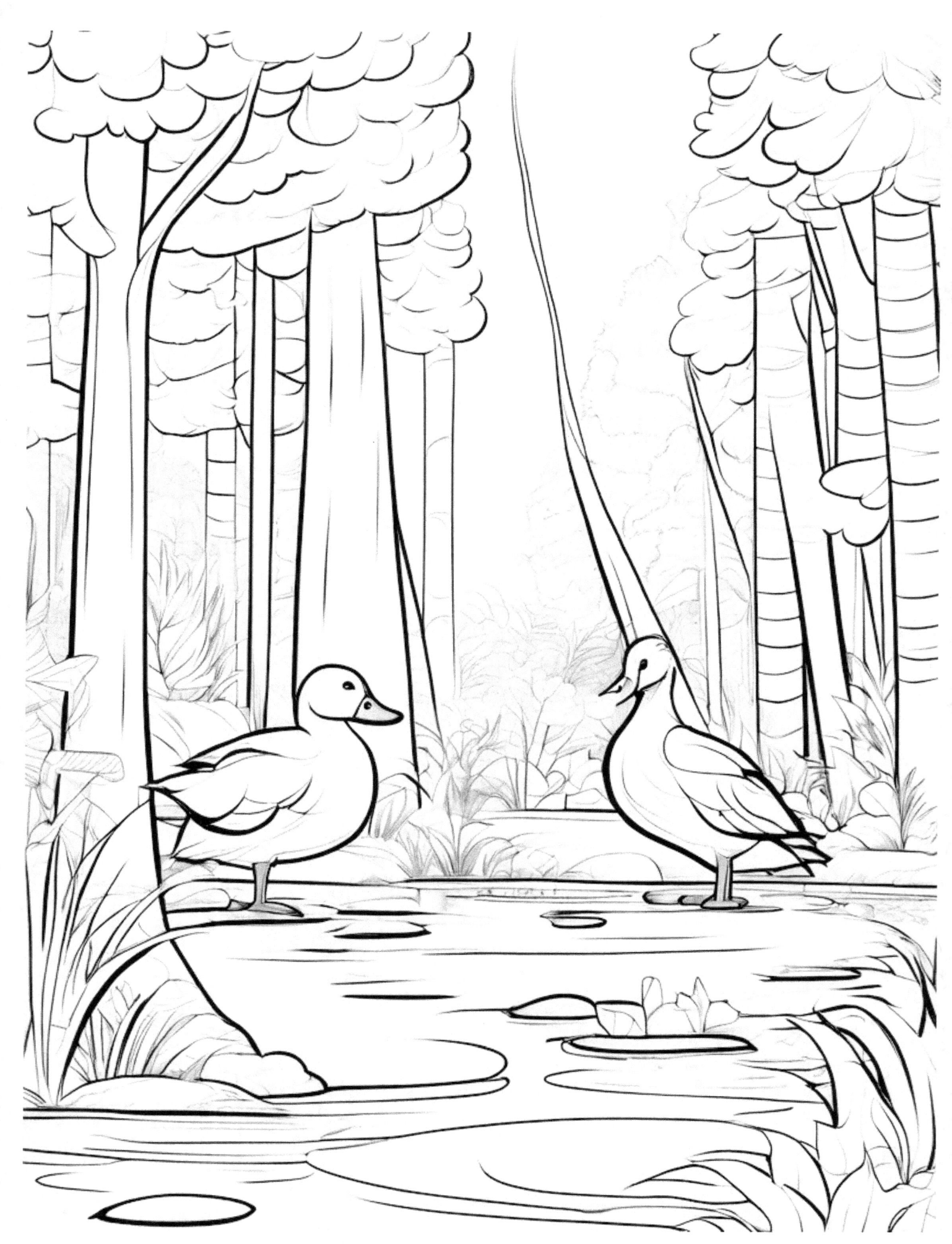

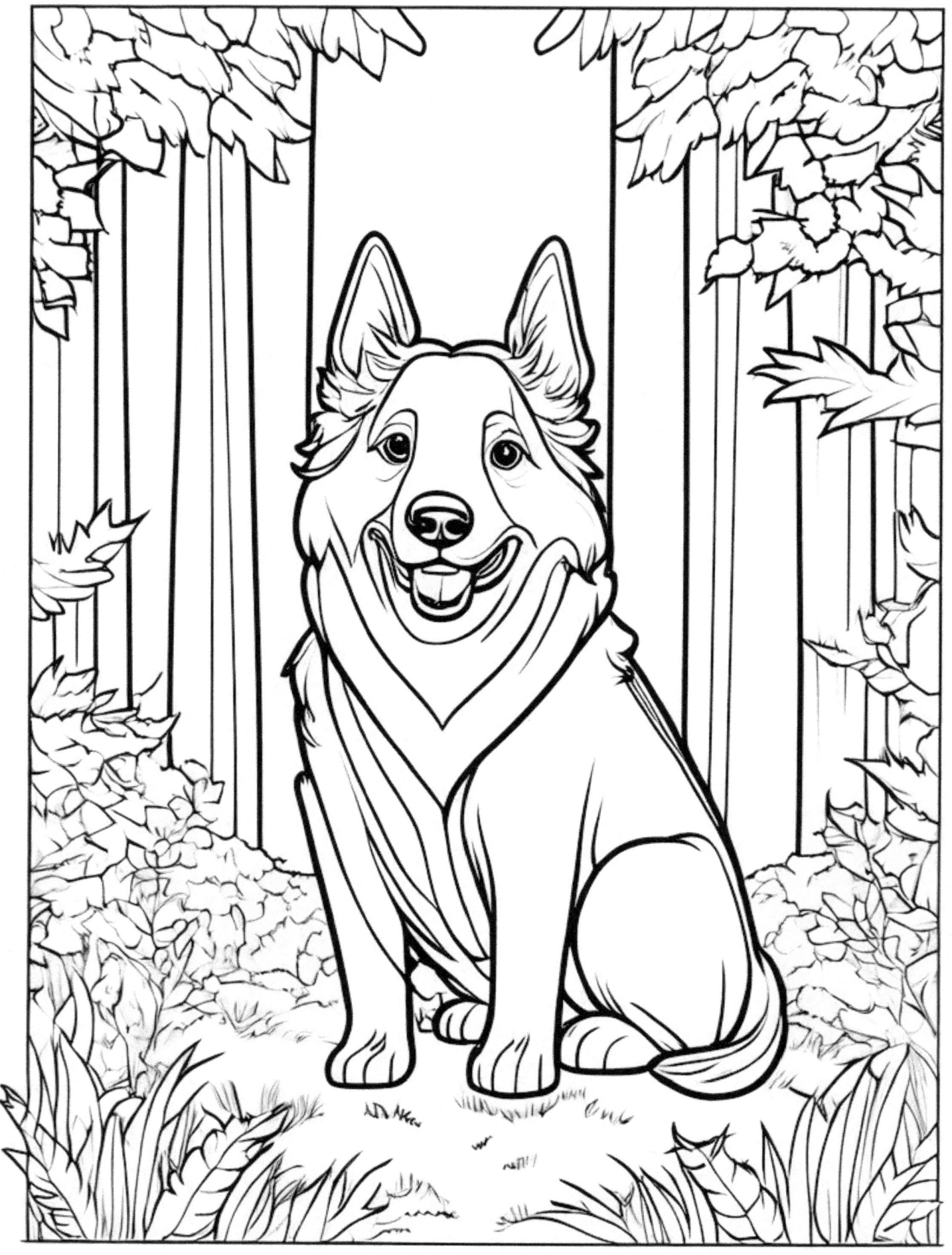

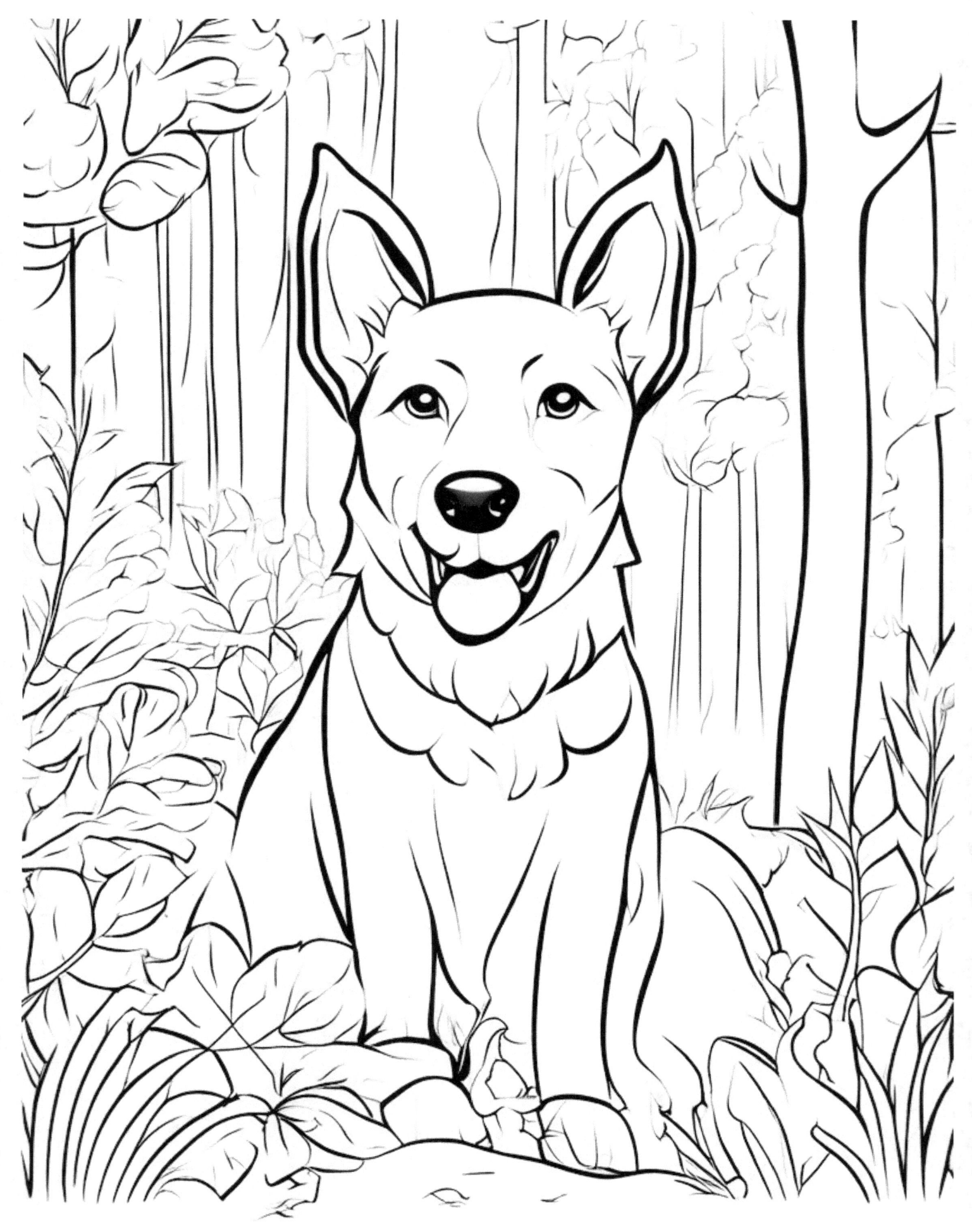

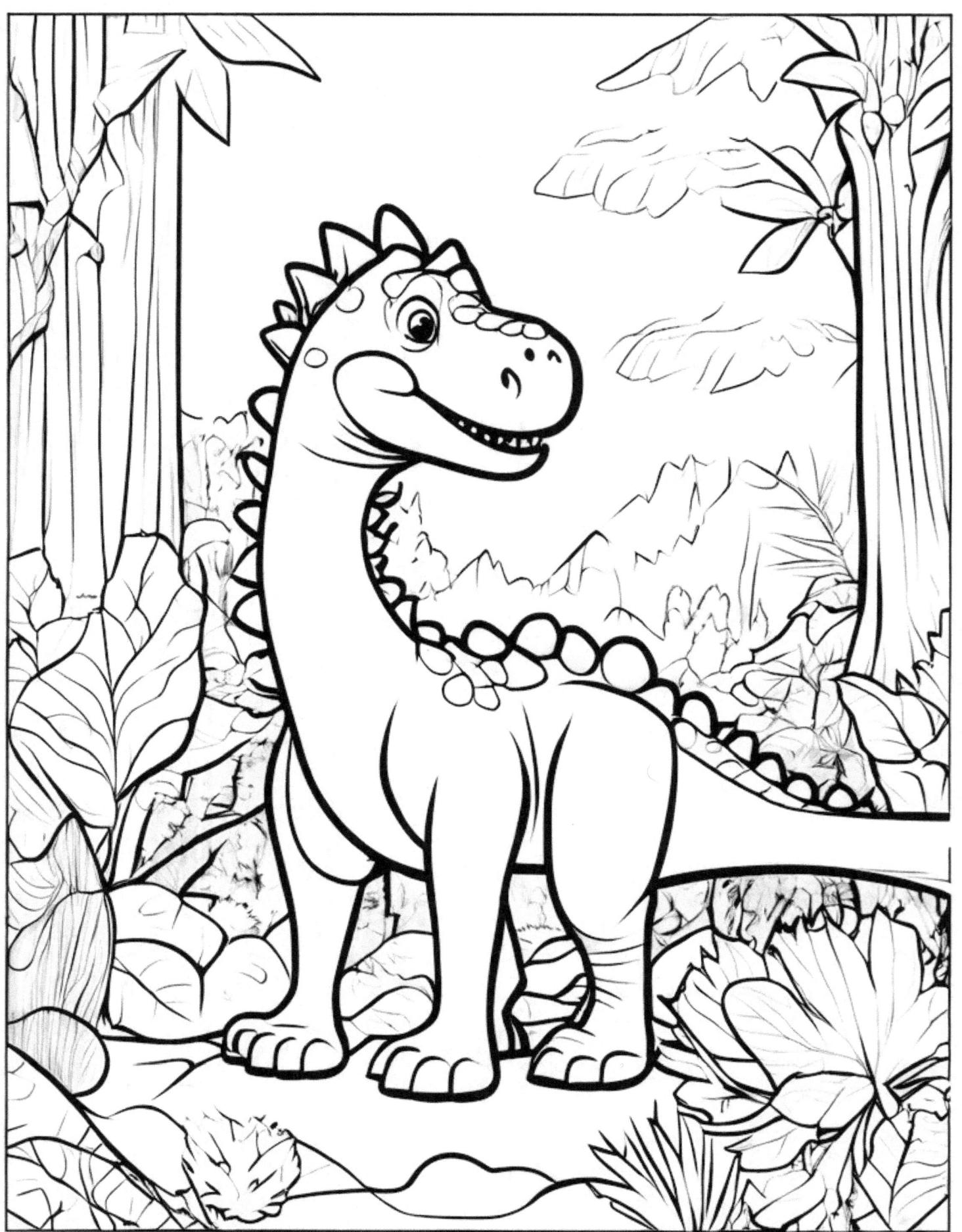

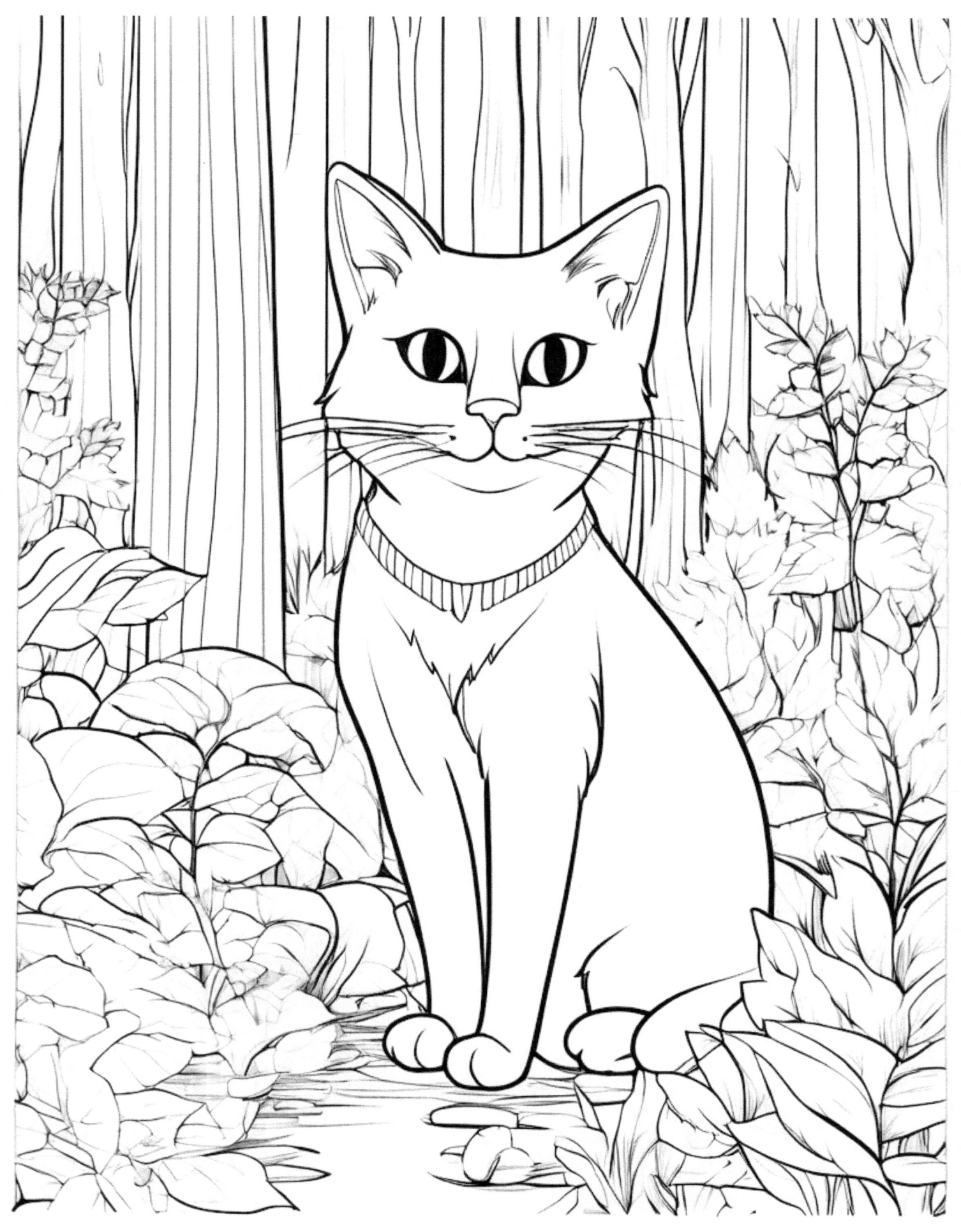

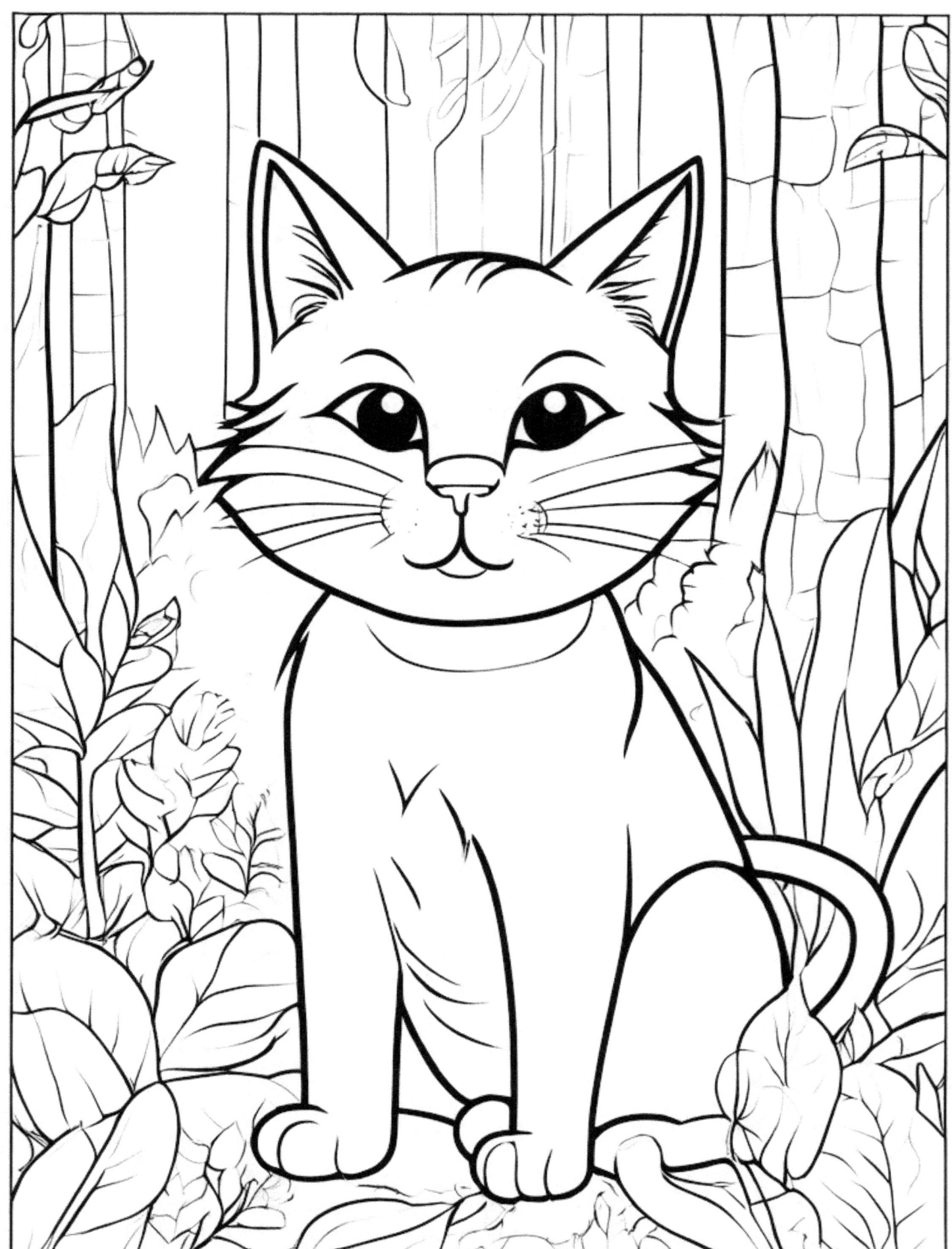

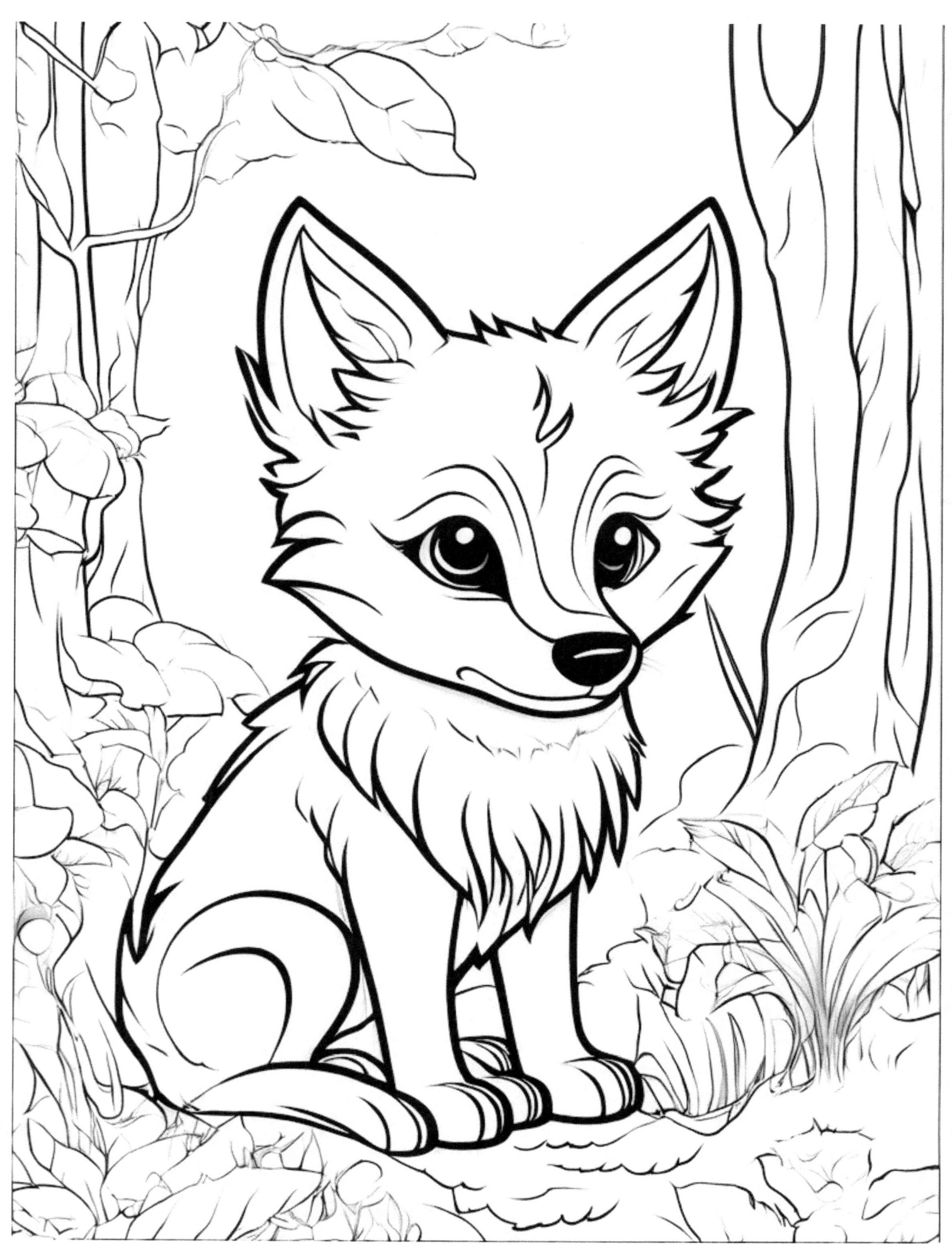

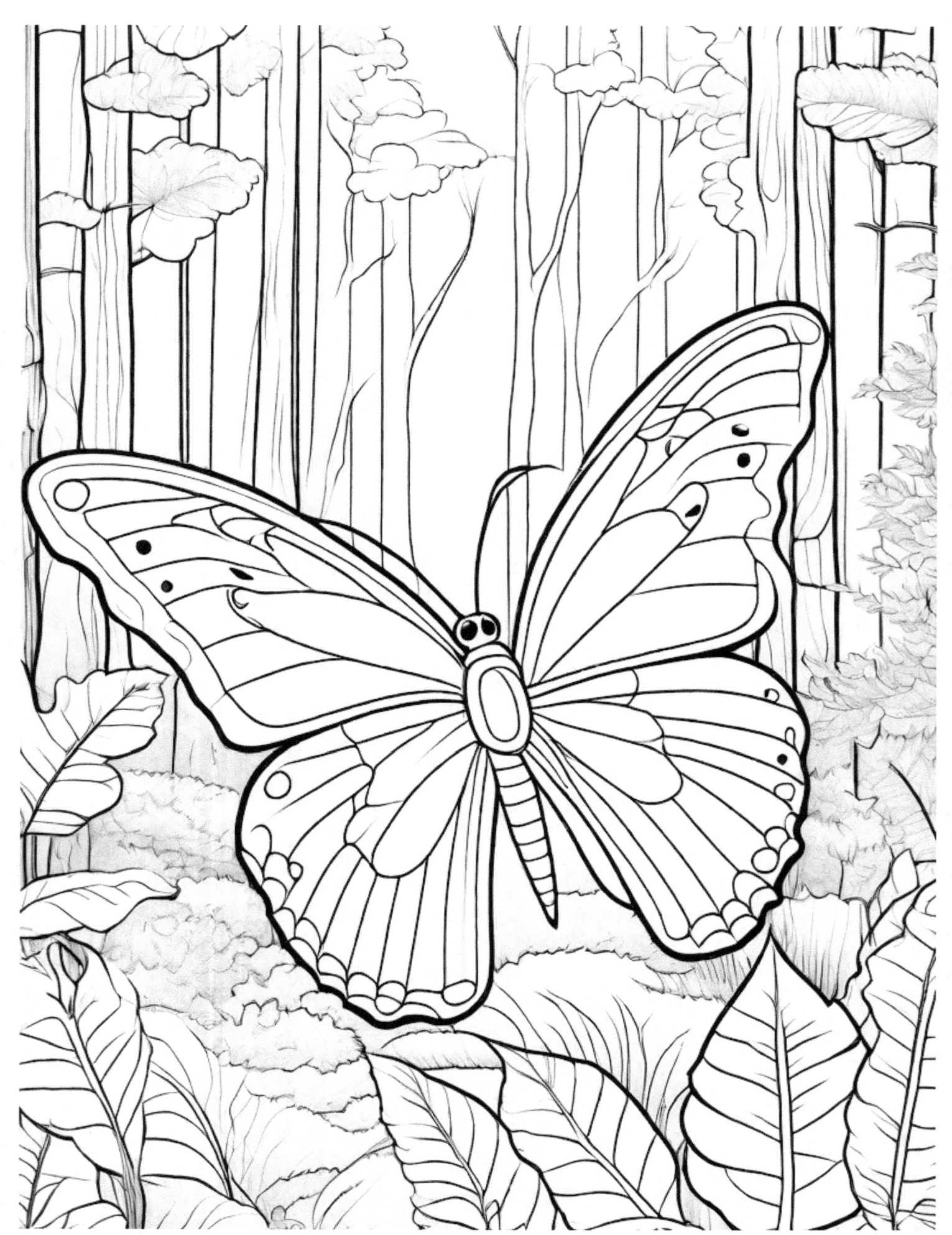

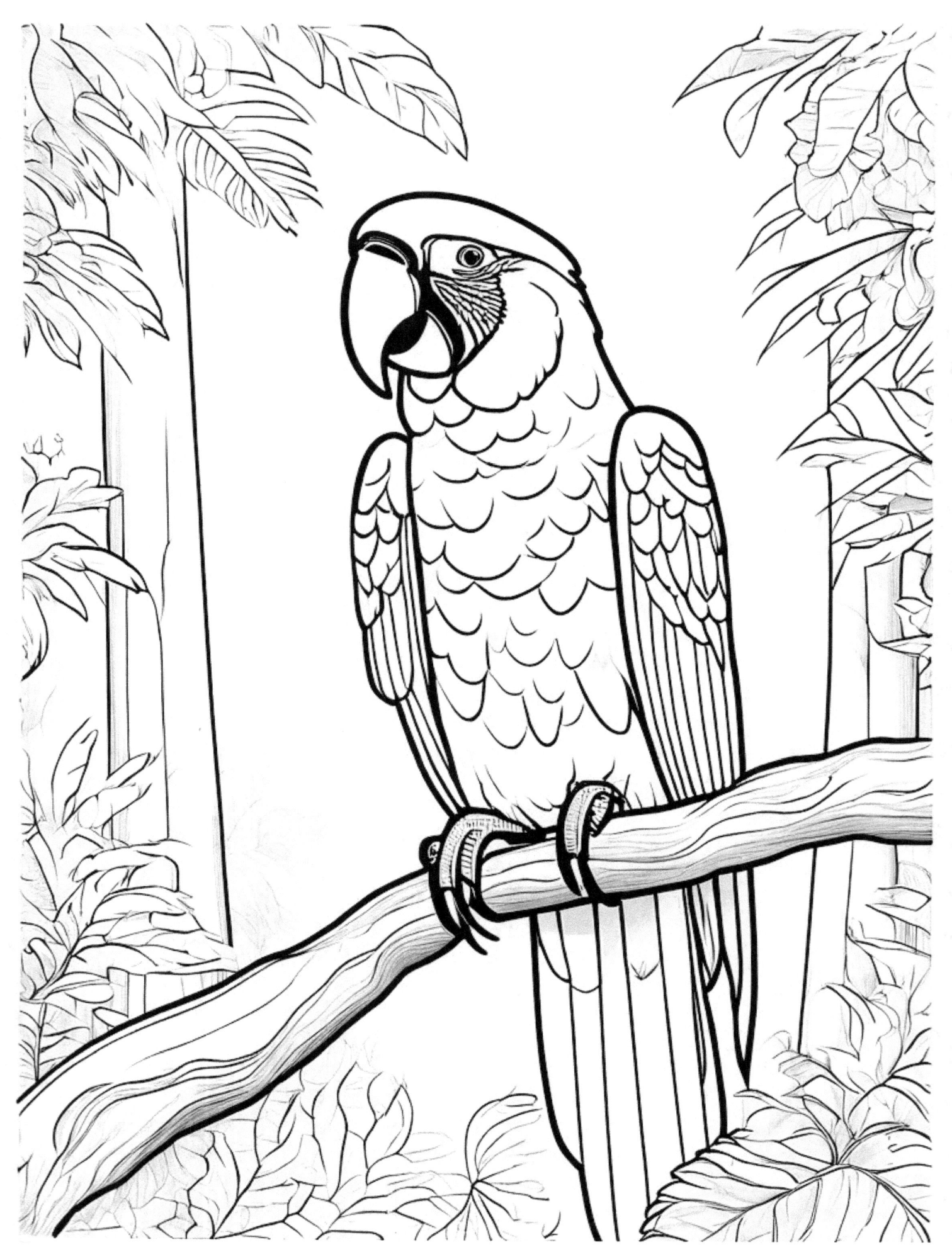

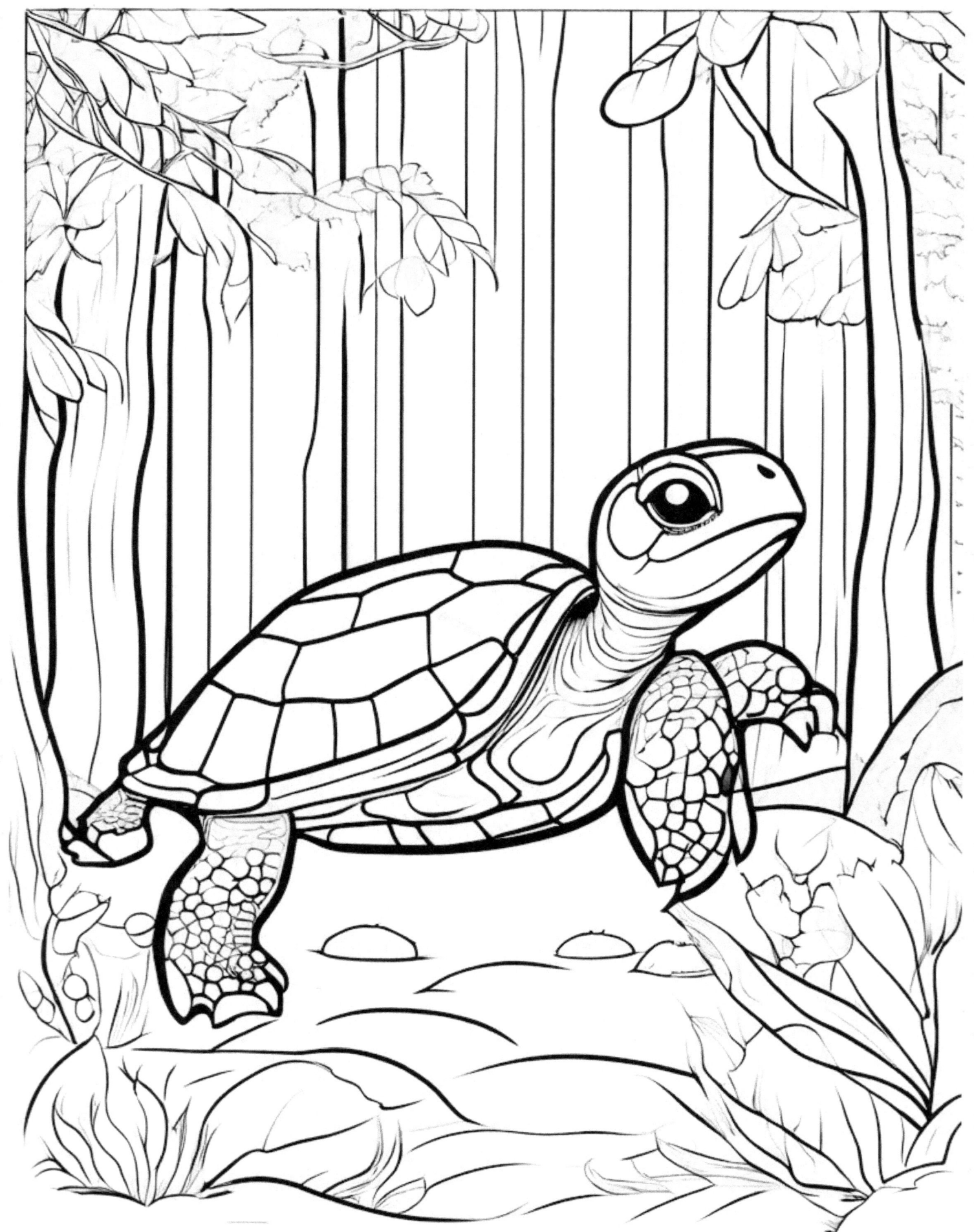

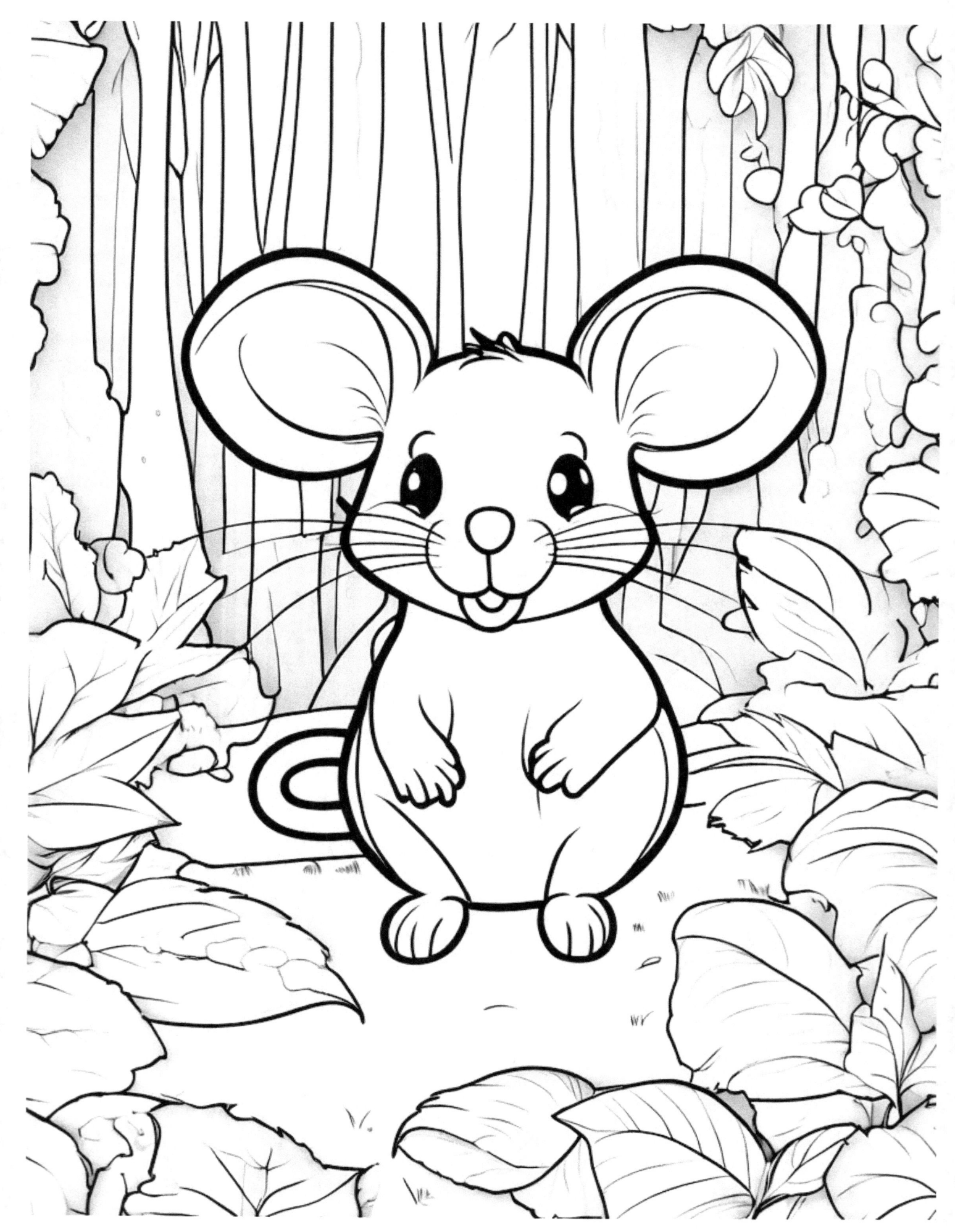

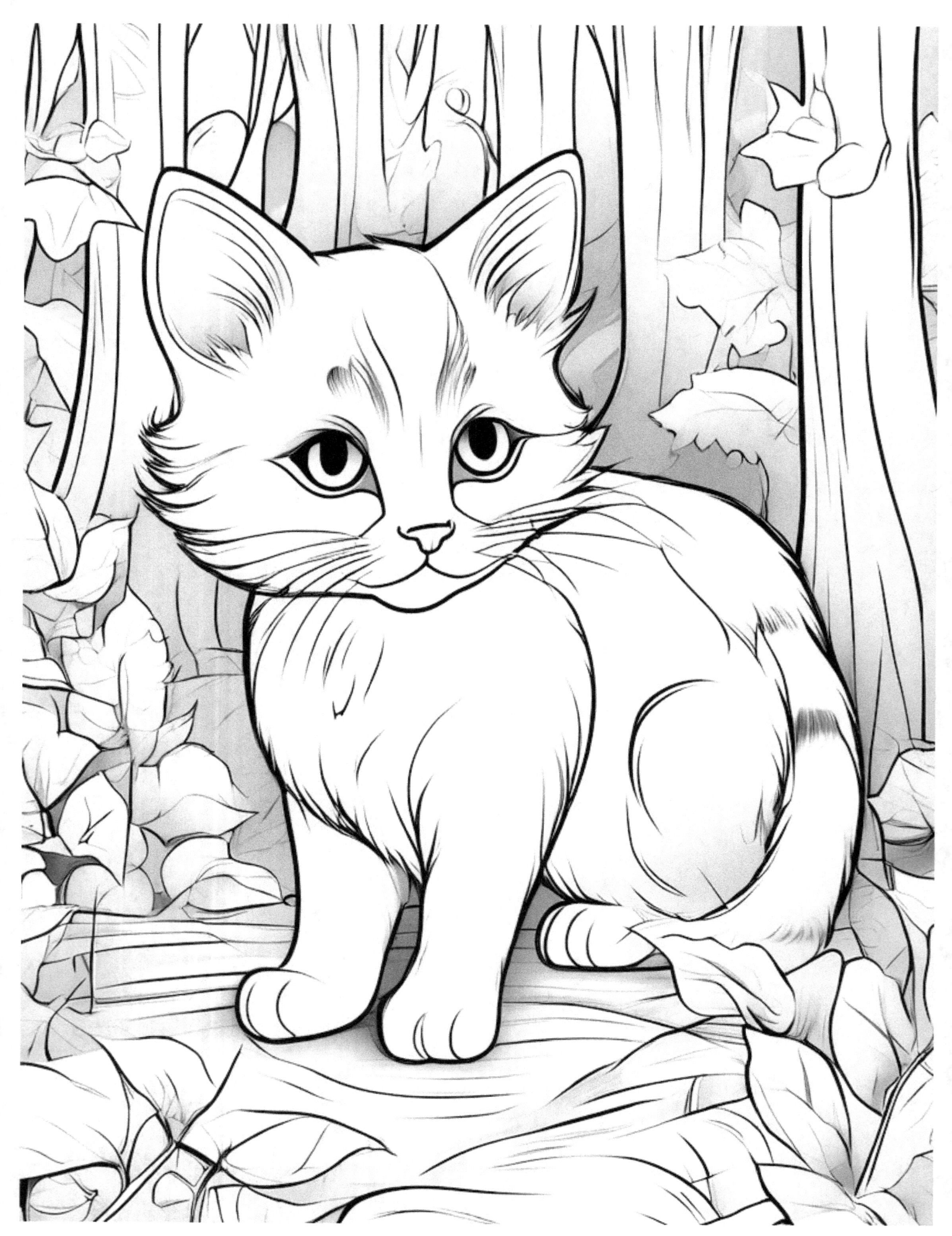

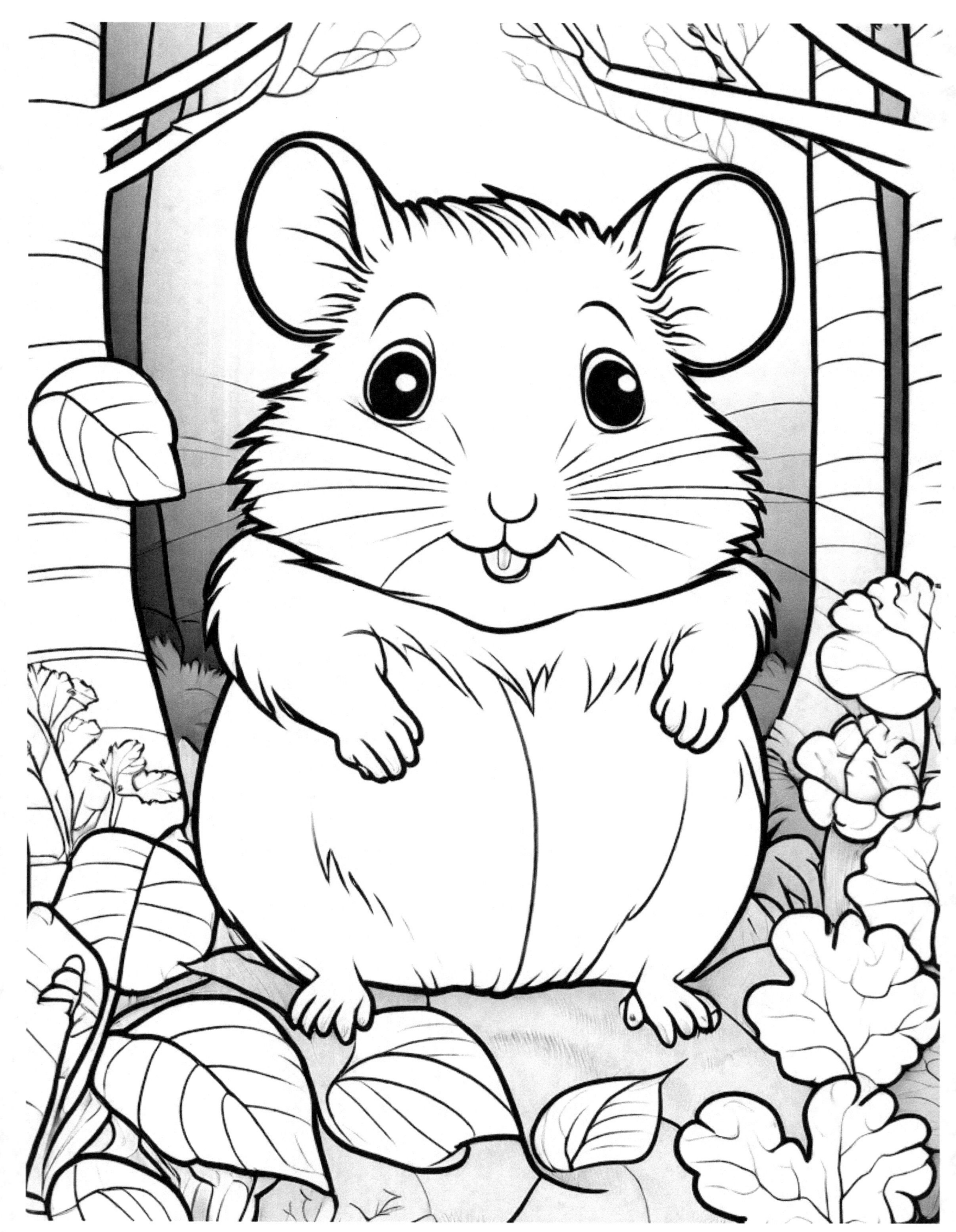

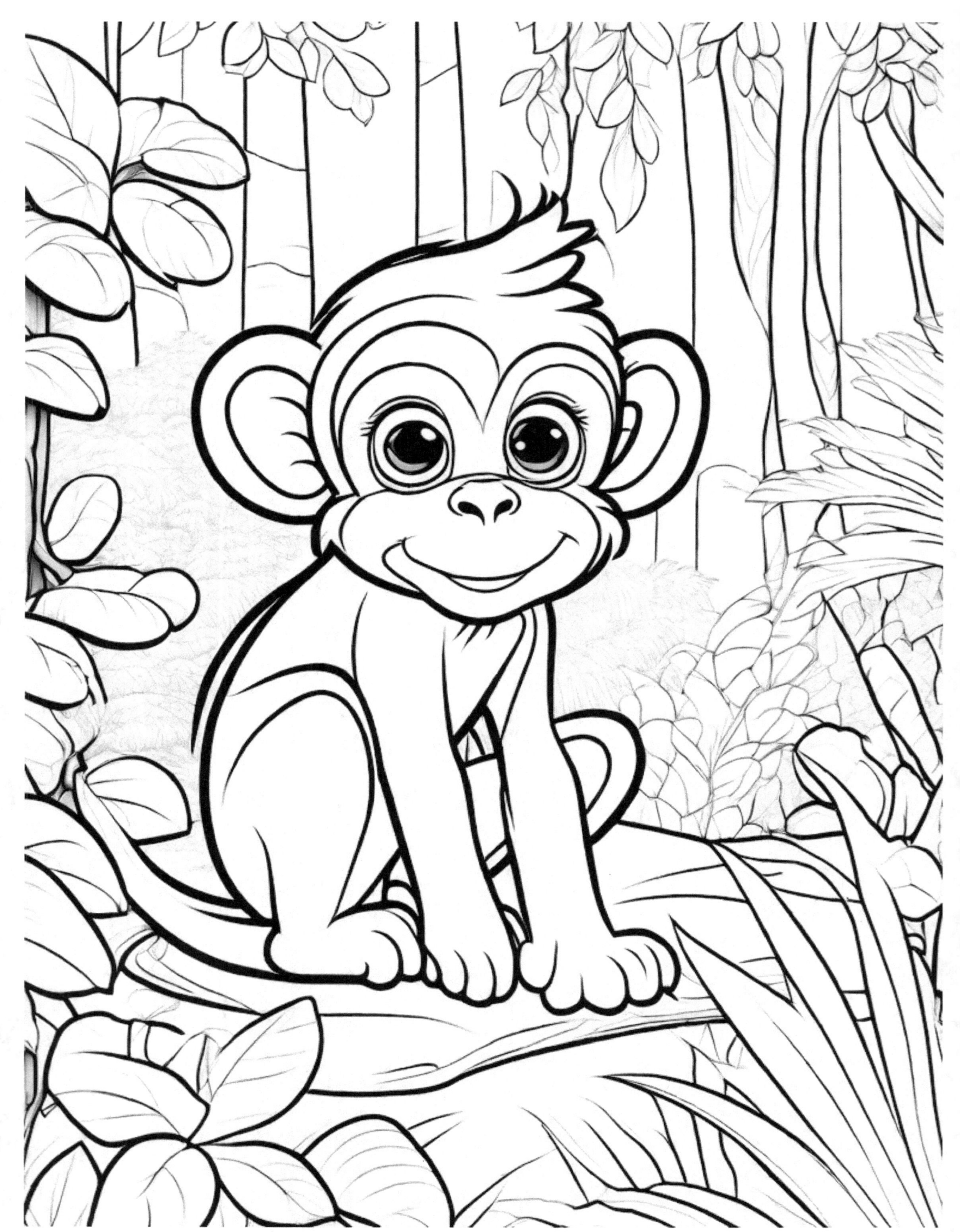

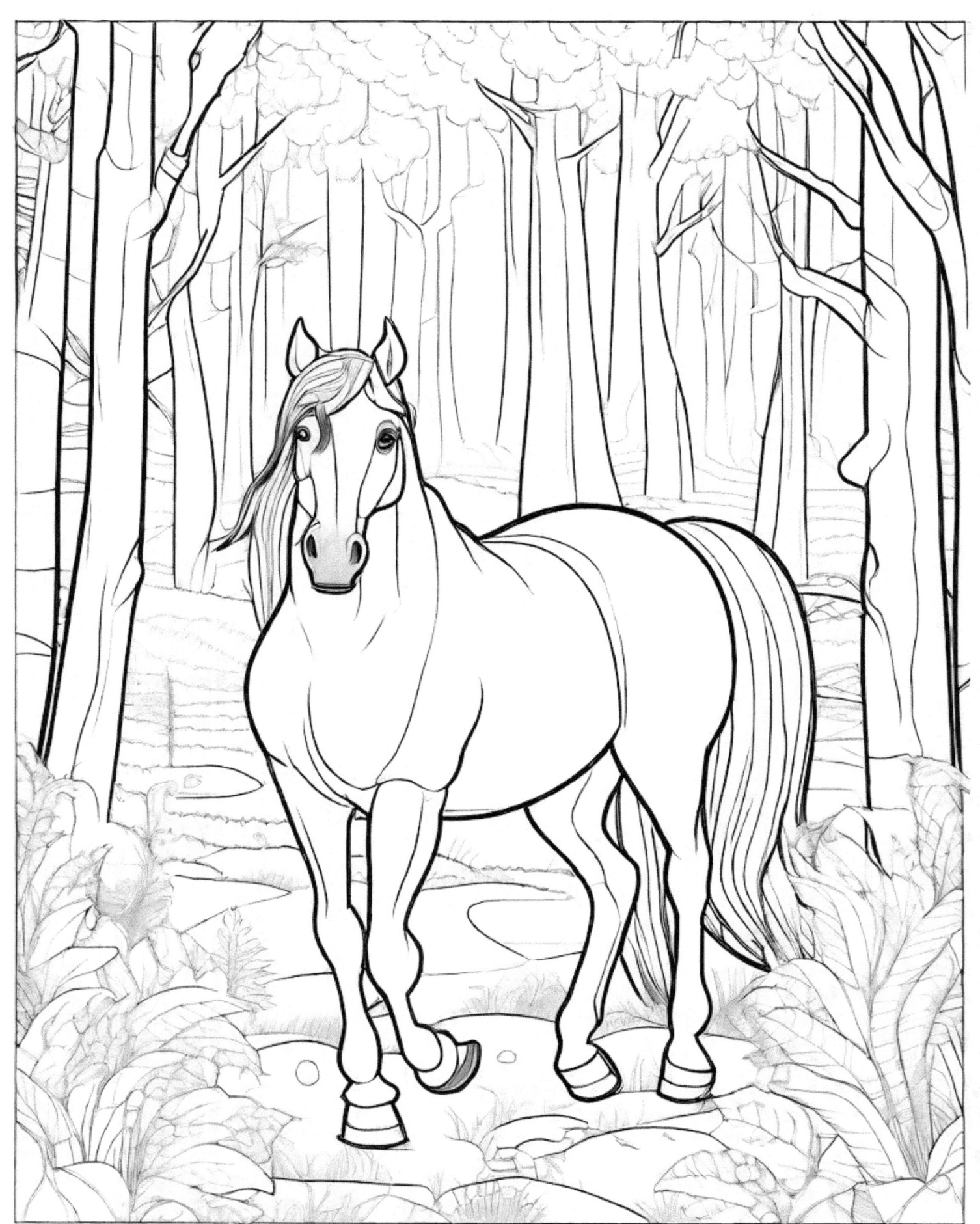

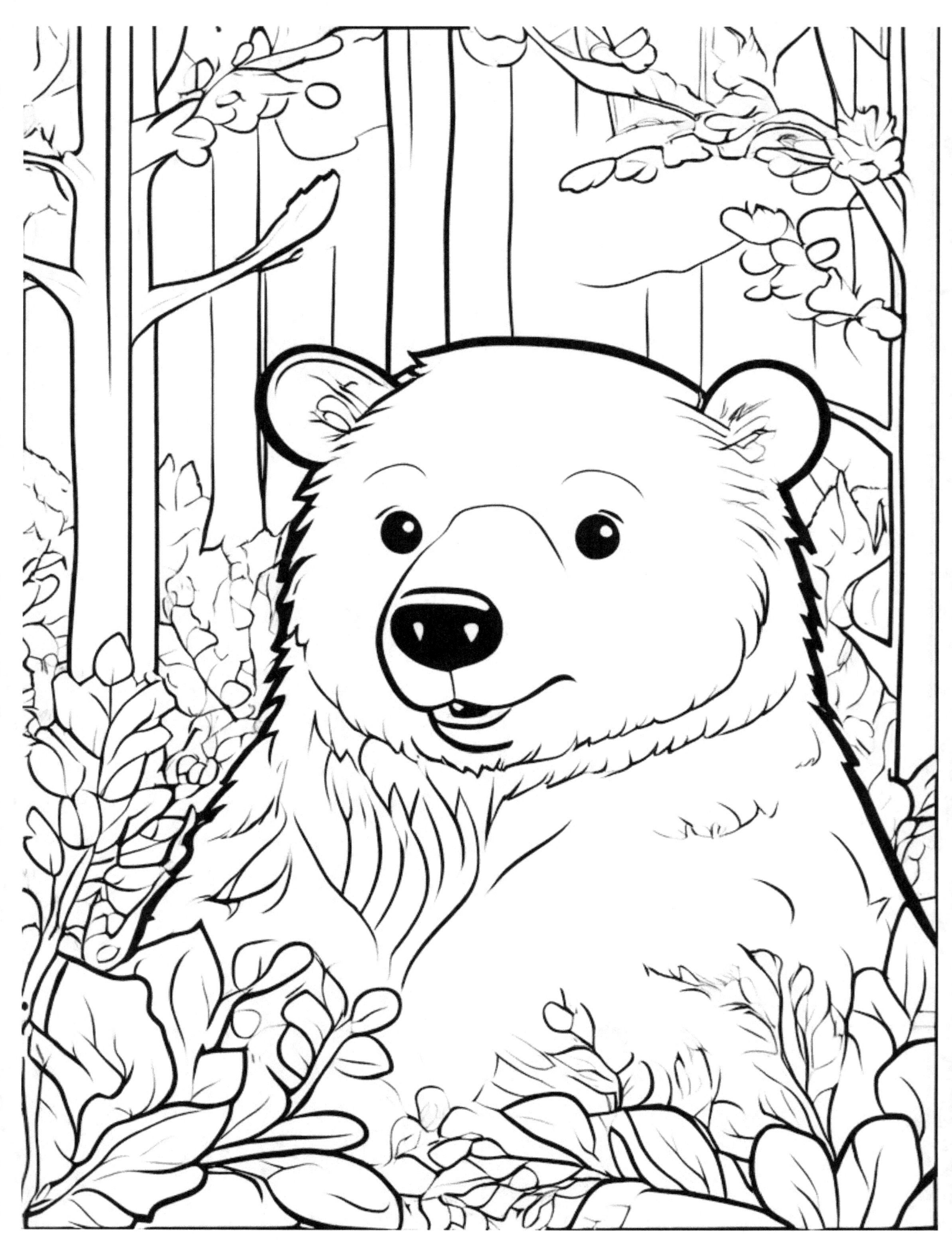

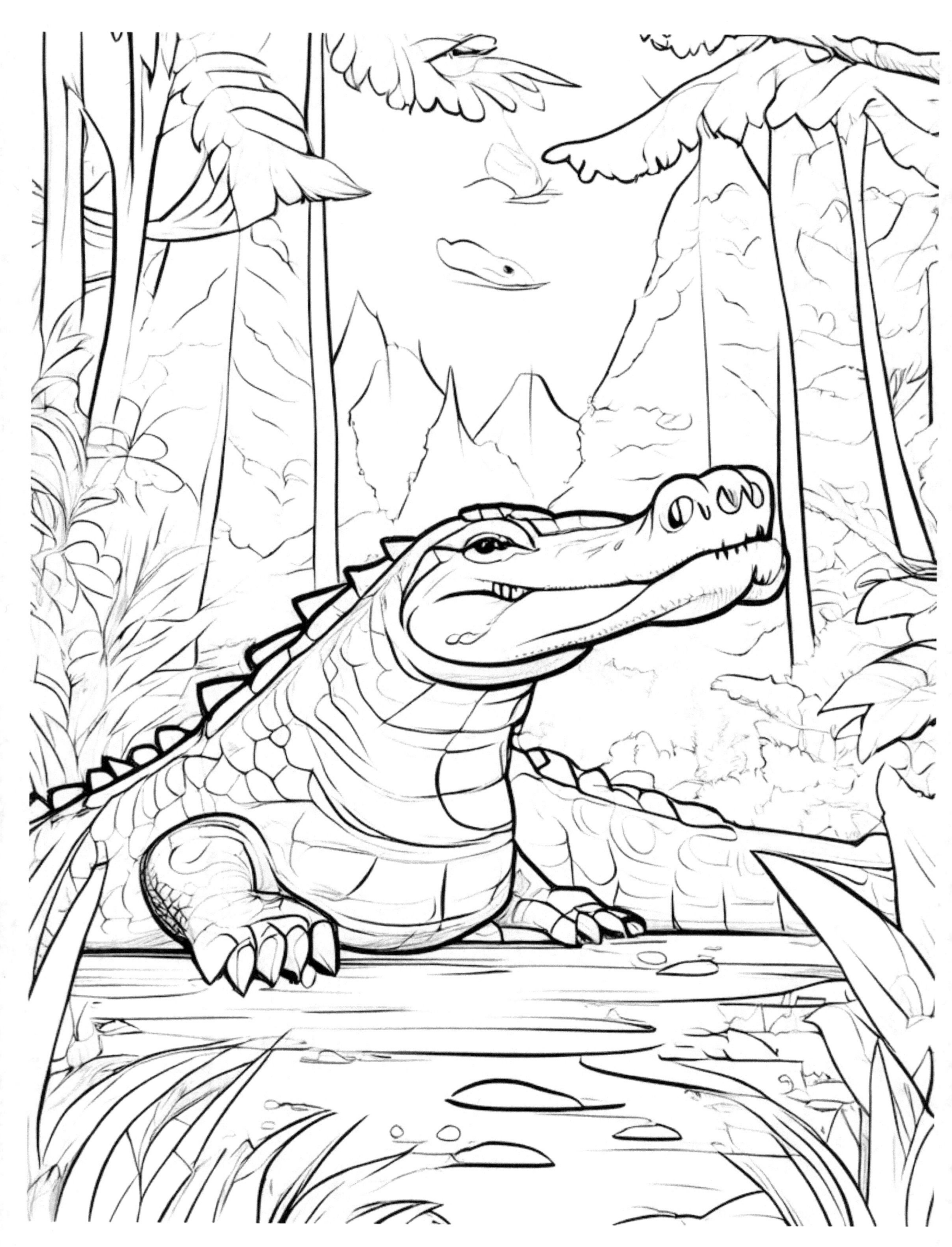

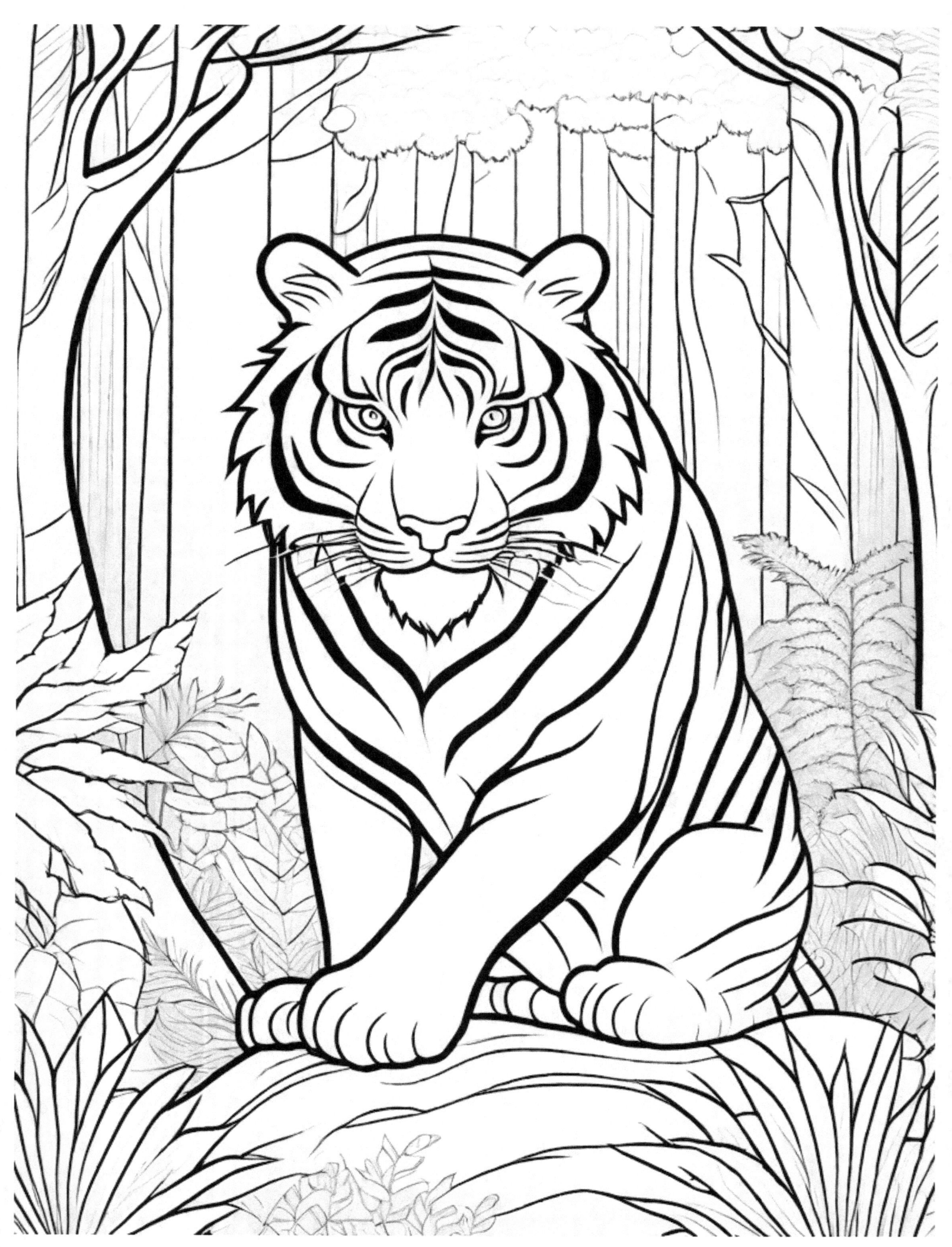

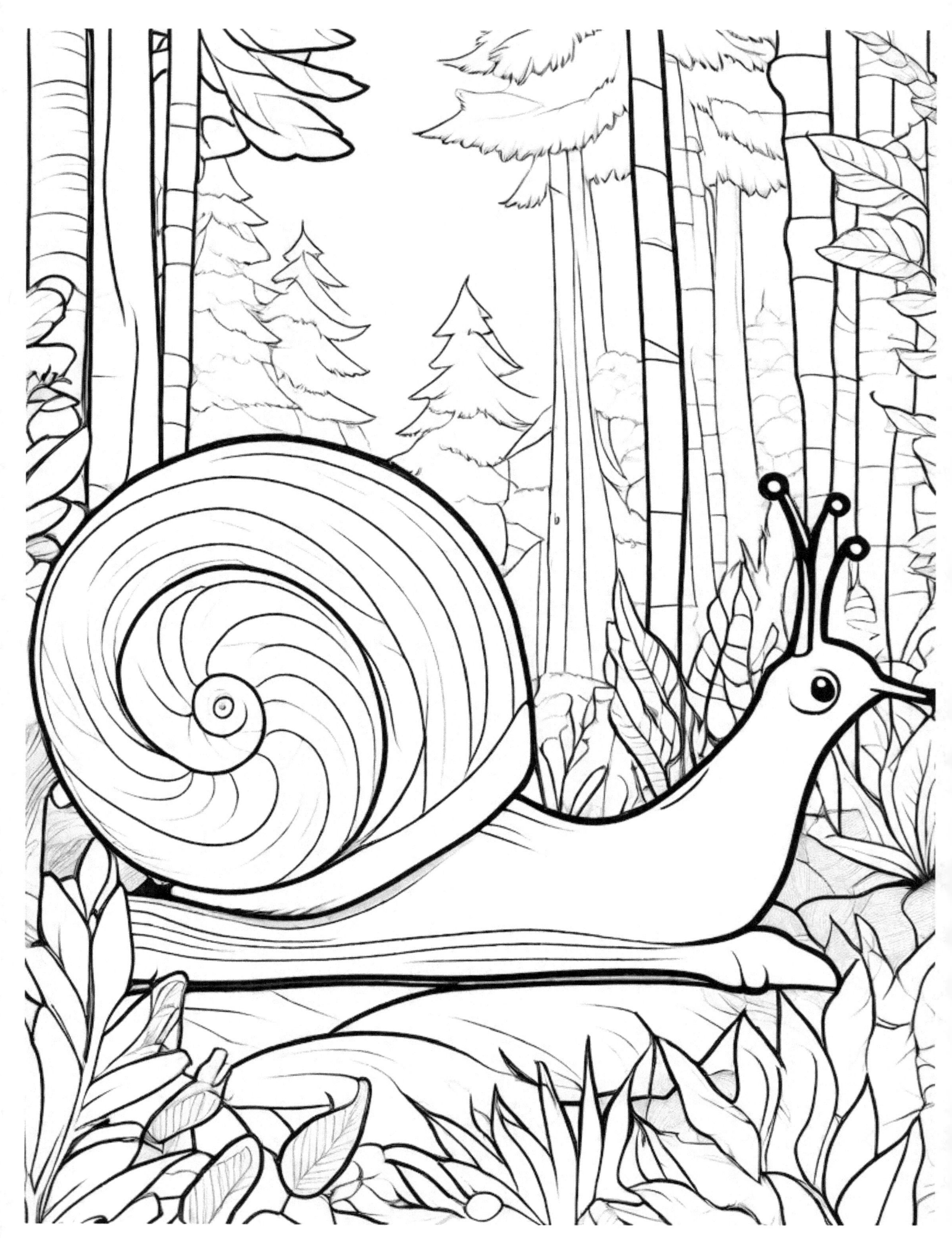

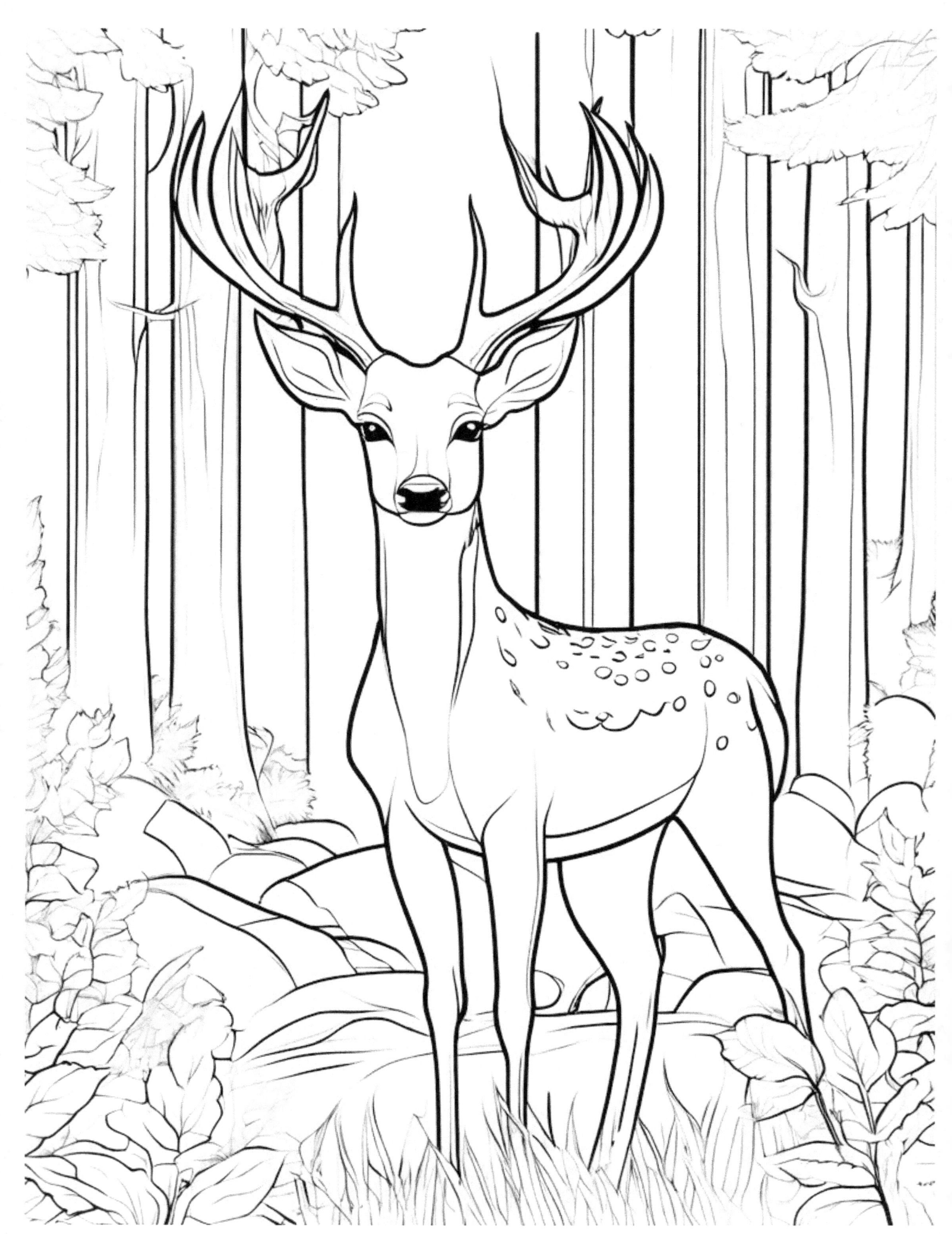

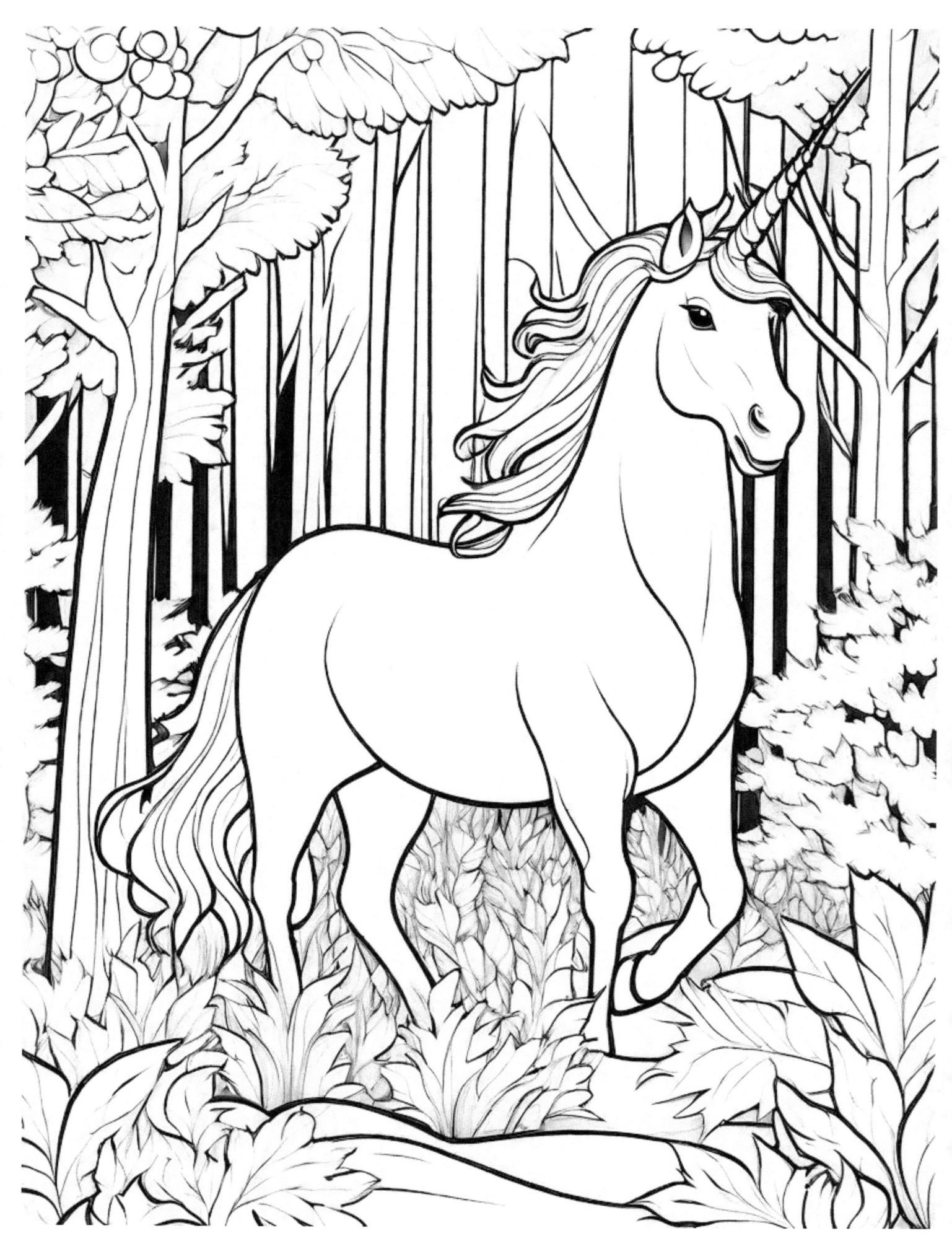

Enhanced:
May your serenity endure, allowing mine to flourish. This tome was crafted with boundless affection and meticulous attention for all who grace its pages.

www.ingramcontent.com/pod-product-compliance
Lightning Source LLC
Chambersburg PA
CBHW062120220526
45471CB00010B/3813